To my old [...] ecol [...]
Don [...] vicar.

Hornby

London 19th April 1989.

GALINA BREZHNEV AND HER GYPSY LOVER

GALINA BREZHNEV AND HER GYPSY LOVER

Stanley Laudan

Quartet Books
London   New York

First published by Quartet Books Limited 1989
A member of the Namara Group
27/29 Goodge Street
London W1P 1FD

Copyright © Stanley Laudan 1989

British Library Cataloguing in Publication Data

Laudan, Stanley
 Galina Brezhnev and her gypsy lover.
 1. Soviet Union. Corruption.
 I. Title
 364.1'323'0947

ISBN 0 7043 2712 0

Typeset by MC Typeset Limited, Gillingham, Kent
Printed and bound in Great Britain by
The Camelot Press plc, Southampton

For Ulla

ONE

Even if Gorbachev swore on his birthmark that I'd be safe, I still wouldn't go. I've escaped from Russia twice already and that's enough for any man.

My first return to Russia was a kind of madness, but the simple truth was that I had the opportunity to go and a mixture of nostalgia and curiosity did the rest. It was a big decision to take in such an impetuous way but, once taken, I felt a sort of relief.

What was Russia like now? Would anyone remember me? I hoped not. Would I recognize anyone? I hoped not. In the days before I left for Moscow my mind filled with the memories of that other time, so many of them unpleasant that I began to wonder why I wanted to go back at all.

Pictures flashed on that screen behind the eyes as I remembered the bad old days. I saw the German tanks brushing aside our feeble Polish resistance as they overran Cracow. Someone shouted, 'Run!' and I remembered how we ran. Rifles can't hurt tanks. But there were some nice pictures. I saw faces long forgotten, faces of my band, faces in our audiences, laughing faces, and once again I revelled in the applause for the songs we used to play. They were my songs and I was young again.

I saw it all again and I wanted it all back. But then I remembered the wire and the half-frightened faces behind the rifle-butts which drove us into the camps.

My heart thudded almost as much as it did when I escaped into the Russian zone. Now the faces were different – some almost Chinese. More wire around another camp.

I remembered the face which first suggested that I form a show band to tour Russia to 'lift morale'. Now the faces were different, but the applause was the same. I saw most of Russia from the west to Vladivostok, from Siberia to Central Asia. I was famous again – and by Russian standards wealthy. With fame came women, fanatical and idolizing, for we were as famous as the Beatles in our way. They flung flowers and items of underwear on to the stage in the Hall of Columns. It seemed funny to think of those willing young bodies, grandmothers now.

Amid those memories of fame and fortune, however, were the faces of those who had denied me freedom; the faces of the KGB of thirty years ago, the faces of the commissars, the faces of the guards – you could call them nothing else – who went with us on all our tours. And as I remembered this part of the past my heart filled again with the despair of being refused permission to join General Anders and his newly-formed Polish Army. The Russians would release all the Poles they held to go and fight the Germans – except, it seemed, me. My pulse beat afresh as I remembered my escape in the spring of 1942 into Persia and the journey with the rest of the Free Poles to Italy. A monastery high, high on a hill, and a terrible pain at a place with a bullet-riddled sign marked Monte Cassino. And after the pain, happy memories of cool beds in British hospitals and kind faces, and the end of the war.*

As my return drew closer and closer, I would wake up in a sweat with one face clear in my mind: the face of Major Rubinzik, whose job had been to keep me

---

*Stanley Laudan's book *The White Baton*, published in 1957, contains the full record of his life inside Russia during those war years.

inside Russia all those years ago. Would he still be alive and waiting for me? I didn't give much for my chances if he were. The red star on his uniform shone through my nightmares.

With all these thoughts popping unbidden into my mind whenever I considered going back, I often felt tempted to withdraw. I dreamed up dozens of excuses but all the time I knew I would go ahead. I wasn't of course foolish enough simply to turn up. I had made a number of Russian contacts in the West in the course of my business as an impresario and my suggestion of a series of tours to the Soviet Union by British artistes had invariably been met with a favourable response, even from the Cultural Department of the Soviet Embassy in London.

All my business sense told me that such tours could be a huge success, probably even greater than the success my band had enjoyed in those days long ago when we had been the first to take modern dance music into the Soviet Union. In doing business with the Russians I had two advantages. First, I spoke fluent Russian. Second, even though the Russians I met may not have heard of me, they all knew my song 'Blue Shawl', which had become a standard in Russia. I was to hear it again many times during my trips to Moscow. It was strange to hear my music and words, born of the misery and heartache of Poles in those wartime days, played and sung in the heartland of Russia, the source of that same unhappiness.

But I am racing ahead of myself. The day of my departure for Russia arrived and my uneasiness increased. I was travelling without even the slim protection of a British passport; all I had was a basic travel document, which did not guarantee protection in any country in the world, let alone Russia. But it was quite clear that the Moscow customs officials had never seen such a document before, and rather than appear ignorant they stamped it hurriedly and waved me through.

There was no doubt that by escaping from Russia during the war – even though I had gone to fight the Germans – I had committed a crime and somewhere there would be a report on my defection to the West. Perhaps it was that bulky file on the desk in front of me? I felt appalled at the stupidity which had led me to place my life in the hands of some official, perhaps at that very moment searching through his dusty files for one marked, 'Laudan, Stanley'. I waited for the hand under my arm, guiding me into that little room at the back of the airport from which I would never return. But nothing like that happened and I went on with Vic Lewis to collect our luggage.

Vic Lewis was the main reason for my returning to Russia. We had common business interests and Vic's agency represented some of my artistes. Vic was very much a VIP. He had just been appointed manager of 'The Beatles' and even the Russians had heard of them.

For Vic this was a business trip, a kind of reconnaissance. He wanted to see his associates in Scandinavia and Denmark but he also wanted to see inside Russia. So we were travelling via Russia to Finland and then on to Denmark. I was to look after him in Russia and sort out the language problems which were bound to arise. At the same time I was to explore the possibility of tours by British artistes to the Soviet Union, confident that some of the performers in my agency would appeal to Soviet popular taste.

Once clear of the airport, I was disappointed. Moscow didn't seem to have changed much. There were a few new modern buildings, like the Rossiya Hotel, but the rest of it was very much the same mixture as before. There were the same multitudes of people, all looking very drab, weaving like snakes along the pavements. There was more traffic than I remembered, but the cars hadn't changed much, except that there weren't so many army trucks. All the cars were black; even the official cars – easy to spot by their flashing lights – were black Chaika sedans.

There were lorries everywhere, just as there had always been. Suddenly I got the feeling that the war was not over. There were lorries in the main streets, in the centre of Moscow, down the side streets, and they all looked as old and decrepit as they had always done. I was back.

After we had booked in at the old National Hotel opposite the Kremlin, the State's Artistic Agency, Gosconcert, took us firmly under their wing, held a variety of auditions for us, and added the obligatory sightseeing tour around Moscow. Vic, however, had his own ideas. To him sightseeing consisted of photography and he would wander off on his own whenever he had the chance. He must have done a great deal of walking on these photographic safaris, because he developed a habit of dropping off to sleep in the middle of the most spirited audition. One evening we were at the Bolshoi in the company of a number of officials from the Ministry of Culture when Vic suddenly toppled sideways and began to snore like a bear. I hit him hard with my elbow. He blinked and looked at me with great surprise and protested, 'I wasn't asleep. I love *Onegin* – I heard every note!' Later I told him that we had been watching *Boris Godunov*.

The next morning while Vic was off on another photographic spree in Red Square I used the opportunity to visit the offices of Gosconcert to talk about my own business. My work in London was pretty varied and my agency represented and promoted a number of artistes, introducing them to recording companies, to television, and making arrangements for concerts.

There was one specific idea I wanted to discuss that morning and I had a particular performer in mind. I had signed him up only a few months before and was quite excited about his future. He was a very promising singer. He had already achieved some minor successes in England and now I thought a concert tour in the Soviet Union would be just the thing to give him experience and the confidence he would need for similar tours in Britain. I knew too that no English singer had performed in the Soviet Union since the war – though there had been singers from Belgium, France and the USA – and that in itself would provide good publicity material.

The singer was Robert Young, and the idea of a Russian tour was very tempting. He was not a pop singer like Tom Jones, but he had a fine voice. He could reach the highest notes like an opera singer and he had already had some experience at club and concert performances in England and would, I thought, cope well with such a tour.

He was also extremely good-looking – or so many women had told me. I grinned to myself at the thought of all that Russian underwear flying over the footlights towards him. I had a lot of faith in him, as did many others in showbusiness, even influential people like the Grades.

With this in mind – and a package under my arm with an assortment of photographs and records of Robert Young singing the sort of songs I knew would appeal to the Russians – I entered the old building at 15 Neglinnaya Street which houses the offices of Gosconcert. It reminded me of an old school, slightly dilapidated, but clean and functional. It was very quiet. When a young girl asked what I wanted, I had difficulty in not whispering the answer.

She went away to find out if the director was able to see me. A door closed behind her and I looked round. This was the Moscow office which had organized my life during the war. Instructions from this very spot had given me the chance to earn my daily black bread all those years ago. It was here that I got my big break in Russian showbusiness!

I didn't have long to savour the memory. The girl was back almost as soon as she had gone to say that the director, a Mr Aleschenko, would see me. I walked into a large bright room with a big desk directly opposite the door. The man behind the desk stood up and extended his hand. He looked intelligent, neatly dressed in an office suit, and he smiled politely. But I could almost feel the reserve.

He soon revealed that my visit was not exactly a surprise . . . 'I am Director Aleschenko. I was warned by our people in London that you were coming back and that I might expect a visit from you. How can I help?'

I didn't like the way he said 'coming back' – it sounded too much like voluntary surrender and had the unfortunate implication that I had abandoned all thought of returning to London. But he was very polite and so I plunged straight into a little speech, which I had prepared some time ago for such a moment. The Russians are hugely sentimental about their country and it is rarely a mistake to praise Russia and the Russian people. An excess of flattery should be avoided, but they do like to hear more than the average Englishman would tolerate.

I started by telling him how nostalgic I had been about Russia and how highly I regarded the Russian people. I chose my words carefully and made them sound as if they came from the heart. He suddenly interrupted me, 'Oh yes, we all know your famous song "Blue Shawl" which you first performed on Russian soil. It is part of our heritage now. We also know that you like the Russian people – why else would you have returned to us?'

I wondered if he was being sarcastic, but ploughed on and showed him all the publicity material about Robert and came straight out with the suggestion of a concert tour for him in Russia. 'Very interesting,' said Aleschenko, as he glanced through the material, 'but you should know perhaps better than anyone that there are certain regulations . . .'

Of course I did, but this first reaction was very disappointing.

'You know that I cannot engage an artiste from the West just like that! I do not even know his style or his repertoire . . . and you know his repertoire will be the most important thing. What words will be delivered from the stage to our people? There are a thousand things to check . . .'

This time I interrupted him. 'Director, who would know better than I what kind of songs and material he should use . . . surely my experience . . .?'

'Things have changed. Not too much, perhaps, but there have been changes . . .' He paused and I thought it was all over. Then he looked straight at me and said, 'All right. I'll tell you what I will do. I will send you to see Mr Golovin. I'll go this far – you can tell him that in principle I have nothing against it, but everything must be done according to the rules.'

I tried not to let my delight show. I knew Golovin quite well. I had met him in London on several occasions and his knowledge of the West would make negotiations with him that much easier. However, my first contact with Golovin in Russia was disconcerting. This was a different man from the one I had met in London. He showed no emotion whatsoever. I could have been a complete stranger. Even his handshake was cool and little more than perfunctory. His opening words were blunt: 'Please, don't let's have any of those phrases and slogans about love and friendship. You want to do business? Then let's talk . . .' But despite his distant attitude, he showed immediate interest in the idea of a Robert Young tour of Russia. He had a habit of mumbling which made him difficult to follow, but he went further than I had ever hoped.

'So you want to be our partner in London, do you? You want to bring English shows to us. All right, I'll help you, but it is not going to be easy. First of all you will have to arrange a performance in London for our ambassador and his staff . . . How many shows do you have in mind? You'll have to bring your own musicians . . . And then, of course, there is the price. What sort of figure do you have in mind?'

As I hesitated, he mumbled on. 'Never mind, we can leave that until later, till after the embassy show. We can talk on the telephone then. I will inform our cultural attaché of any decision . . .'

I thanked him and his last words were, 'I'll see you here in Russia very soon.' He seemed so sure about it. In fact I had a telephone call from him the next day and our reunion was indeed 'very soon' – he had arranged a meeting with 'some important people from the Ministry of Culture' in an hour's time!

Vic Lewis and I were ushered into a room at the ministry dominated by a huge oval table. Once my eyes had got past that, I saw a row of faces, each betraying its Party member and KGB status. The man in charge was different. He was blue-eyed and dressed in a modest blue suit, but the air of authority he exuded from his place at the head of the table had to be felt to be believed. I knew that old twinge of fear from earlier days in Russia and almost spoke my thoughts aloud to Vic Lewis to warn him to be on his guard. This man was a big fish.

He introduced himself politely but firmly: 'Alexander Ivanovich Supagin, Head of the Foreign Relations Department of the Ministry of Culture.' He presented the others – two men and a woman – and then without warning asked me, 'So you know Russia well, Gospodin Laudan? I am told you have read Lenin and Marx, is that so?' It was more the tone than the question that made me angry.

'Yes,' I said. 'I have read Marx – and *Mein Kampf* – and the Holy Bible. I have read a lot of books. I like reading.'

It was clear that neither my anger nor my response surprised him. He looked at his colleagues and smiled. He sounded very much like a benign schoolmaster when he said, 'I am very pleased with your answer. You see, we do not think much of the people who come to the Soviet Union as tourists or businessmen and try to flatter us all the time, trying to make us believe they like everything about us, and sometimes even giving the impression that they are practising Communists in their own country when we know it is not so. We call them "sitting-room Communists". They are not aware of even the most elementary facts!' There was some anger in his own voice when he spoke of 'sitting-room Communists' and I wondered who had upset him.

It couldn't have been poor Vic, who sat there while all this was going on unable to understand a word. Supagin then gestured to one of the men and out came the vodka, which was a very good sign. The Russians have a saying that they only drink with someone they like and trust, and now the toast was to 'co-operation and friendship'. We were accepted. So far.

Vic and I left Russia via Leningrad for Helsinki, but none too smoothly. The customs officials at Leningrad turned out to be particularly nasty specimens. They turned our suitcases inside out and then we had to submit to a rigorous body check. I told the officer in charge that we were honoured guests of the Soviet Union, mentioning every top name I could think of. 'Our duty is to check everybody, no matter who they are,' he said, and added that they were looking for icons.

'You're searching the wrong person. I'm not religious,' I said.

'That's got nothing to do with it. Icons are old and valuable treasure and smugglers sell them for a great deal of money in the West. Because of smuggling there are fewer and fewer icons left in Russia.'

They finally let us go and we arrived home safely. I

hadn't been back long when I ran into an icon 'smuggler'. I was in a car with Dimitri Tiomkin on our way back from a meeting when he asked me how my Russian trip had gone. I told him and added the details about the customs at Leningrad. He burst out laughing. Dimitri is of Russian descent and one of the richest composers in the world: 'High Noon' alone brought him around $7,000,000 in royalties and he had just finished work on a film life of Tchaikovsky. I thought he would never stop laughing about my Leningrad incident. 'My dear boy,' he spluttered, 'you have suffered for the sins of others. I took a lot of icons out of Russia. I bought them for next to nothing and sold some for a fortune. Onassis paid me $80,000 for one. You see, I had to travel backwards and forwards between the States and Russia for filming and I had to find some way of getting my costs back. After all, you know yourself how tight-fisted the Russians are . . .'

I did indeed. Although the show at the embassy had been a great success – almost a formality really – the contract I had signed with the Russians was certainly not very satisfactory from a financial point of view. But it was a beginning.

— TWO

Robert Young was an enormous success in Russia, although on the first tour we suffered every inconvenience that Russian bureaucracy can place in the way of a traveller: poor food, officious officials, interpreters who are really spies and accommodation that made the worst British bed-and-breakfast look like the Ritz. But the tour was a huge success and Robert was invited back.

On the second tour women mobbed him and on his third visit, tickets for his concerts were changing hands on the black market at twenty times their face value. I used to find it exhilarating to peep from behind the curtain backstage at those high-paying audiences as they filed into their seats. We had a hole in the scenery which was used to gauge audience reaction. It was from here that I first set eyes on the man who was to make my time in Russia hopelessly insecure. He was Boris Buryatsa, the gypsy lover of Brezhnev's daughter.

The Rossiya Concert Hall in Moscow was filled to capacity that night, just as it had been for the previous three shows. There were six scheduled for Moscow before we were to leave on tour. The Rossiya Hotel is a complex including the concert hall and is one of the most modern and attractive features of contemporary Moscow. The view at night from the panoramic restaurant on the twenty-first floor is breathtaking. Despite the food – so bad it was barely edible – and the typically poor Russian service, it was almost impossible to get a seat any night of the week. I used to think that England provided the worst waiters in the world but the average Russian waiter is in a class by himself.

The concert hall in which we were performing is very beautiful. It has spacious foyers floored with marble under crystal chandeliers, parquet floors, chrome barriers and large mirrors everywhere. Far from being forbidding, it has character and warmth. The hall seats over 3,000 people on comfortable velvet-covered seats into which loudspeakers have been discreetly set to give first-class sound. But the most impressive feature of the whole hall is that at the push of a button the seats disappear to create a huge dancefloor, while at the same time the chandeliers are lowered to give a beautiful ballroom effect. The Rossiya Concert Hall is one of the smartest in Europe and the public who attend shows there are, by Russian standards, pretty smart too.

That night we were to play our fourth Moscow concert in the Rossiya: the fourth of Robert Young's third tour of the Soviet Union. Everyone had heard of him. His records were played over and over again on Soviet radio. He was a star.

The band struck up and Robert walked out on to a stage covered in flowers, thrown there by his fans before he even started to sing. It was just the right atmosphere for my first setting eyes on the man who was to change my life.

I was standing backstage enjoying the screams and sighs and roars of applause for Robert's magnificent voice when Tola, our compère, said quietly to me, 'Take a look at this! It's unbelievable!' Tola pointed through the hole in the scenery to the middle of the front row. 'He's here again. He's been at every concert since we started the tour. He sits in the same seat each time, but from the way he acts you'd think it was all new to him . . .'

I looked through the small opening and saw him at

once. I can recall my first impression even now. He was everything that a woman would find attractive – dark with a suntan, his teeth showing pearly-white in a broad smile, his eyes shining green in the reflection of the lights from the stage. He wore a black smartly-tailored silk shirt and the edges of the open collar sparkled with jewels. I didn't need to be told that they were real rubies and diamonds – the light bounced from the spotlights focused on Robert Young and made a sparkling ring round the man's neck. He stood out from the audience as if he had come from Mars!

'Who is he?' I whispered to Tola. 'He must be a foreigner.'

'I'm sure he's native,' he said. 'I've watched him – he speaks Russian just like us . . . he looks like a gypsy to me.' Tola was right. He looked just like a romantic novelist's idea of a gypsy prince. I couldn't take my eyes off him. He beamed with health and energy, clapping at Robert's performance and, when I joined Robert on stage for our closing item, he jumped to his feet and shouted, 'Bravo! Bravo!' The woman next to him was attractive, middle-aged, and very well-dressed by Russian standards. He kept telling her in a loud voice how splendid the show was but she, it seemed, had eyes only for Robert Young, who brought the house down with his last song: my own 'Blue Shawl'.

Afterwards, when we sat in Robert's dressing room in the state of euphoria that comes after a successful show, I told Robert that we should be ready with photographs for the mob I knew would be outside, and that I'd arranged for us to have dinner in our rooms later because I knew he'd be a long time getting away from his fans. The short distance from the stage door to the hotel entrance – only a matter of a few yards – often took him an hour or more.

That night was no exception. I saw one woman take Robert's hand and clutch it straight to her breast. Robert only just had time to wink at me before the crowd swallowed him up. I pushed my way through and got my share of compliments, but none like that. Robert was the star, their idol. When I finally broke free I was right in the entrance to the hotel, and I was about to go in when I heard someone call me by name. I turned round. And there he was – the gypsy! He stretched out his hand in a manner that can only be described as ostentatious. His words were just as full-blown: 'Maestro, at last I have the privilege of meeting you!'

The hand which grasped mine sagged under a ridiculously large diamond ring. Round his neck, as well as those rubies and diamonds embroidered into his shirt collar, was a thick gold chain from which hung a gold cross picked out with yet more precious stones. Under his left arm was tucked a small black 'handbag', the sort of travel bag which had been popular among Western men for several years. He gestured with his free hand towards the woman who had been sitting next to him at the concert. 'May I introduce to you Maya Isaakovna. I am Boris Buryatsa. My mother was a gypsy princess and, as you will have noticed, I am keeping up the tradition.' He laughed loudly at his own joke.

In that Moscow street Boris, in all his finery, was quite a sight. A little crowd soon gathered around us. The women in it looked at Boris with a mixture of admiration and envy. Boris carried on as if he was so used to such attention that he did not notice it at all. 'We stopped you so rudely, Maestro . . . please forgive us . . . because we would like to invite you to have dinner with us.'

Boris intrigued me, but I hesitated to break that first rule for all visitors to Russia: don't talk to or accept invitations from strangers. 'I am very sorry, but I am unable to accept your invitation. I have already made other arrangements for tonight.' I don't know why the words came out so pompously but Boris got the message.

'Ah, I know that you people from the West, especially from England, need more warning before being invited anywhere.'

Maya interrupted him and turned to me. 'Why don't you change your arrangements? You can bring Robert with you?'

Boris showed a flash of irritation: 'There's no need to bring Robert – much as I like his voice. I can see him on the stage any time. Indeed I have bought tickets for every night. No, it is you, Maestro, I should like to meet. I feel that we have a lot in common and a great deal to say to one another.'

I was surprised at his way of speaking and alarm bells were going off in my mind. Who is this man? How can he walk around like this? A gypsy, yet obviously so wealthy? Through the alarm bells came another survival rule: don't get involved. You are being watched. Get rid of them. So I said to Boris, 'I am sorry, I can't join you. Maybe tomorrow.' It was intended as a brush-off, but Boris didn't read it like that.

'Tomorrow then. The same time. I'll be here!'

And before I could say anything, he led Maya across the road and into a brand-new Mercedes sports saloon parked right outside the hotel. He roared away with a complete disregard for the traffic coming up behind him. Maya waved from the window and they were gone into the Moscow night.

I found Robert in a private room off the hotel restaurant and tried to talk to him about my meeting with Boris, but he was still absorbed in his success and only really listened when I explained that this man was one of his greatest fans. 'You should have brought him to dinner,' said Robert. 'The woman sounds interesting.' I tried to explain to him, as I did on each trip, about the dangers of accepting casual invitations but he shrugged off the warning as usual.

While we were talking, our interpreter, Natasha, asked if she could join us. Robert immediately supposed she was making a pass at him. 'What a question! Fancy asking if you can join us! As far as I am concerned you can not only join me at the table but in my bed too!'

Natasha blushed, but her answer put a full stop to any further discussion along those lines: 'I am a married woman and if you knew my husband's strength you would not be so unwise as to start anything with me . . . we want you to be fit for the tour, don't we?'

Robert laughed it off: 'Well, some you win, some you lose . . .' and went off to rehearse a new song.

I took the opportunity to ask Natasha if she knew Boris Buryatsa.

'Oh him,' she said casually, but there was a peculiar tone in her voice which intrigued me. I knew that Natasha had been a member of the Komsomol and had then become a full member of the Communist Party. She was married to an ordinary unskilled worker, and that made her an aristocrat of Russian society. She had studied English and French at the Institute of Foreign Languages in Moscow, and had become a top-flight interpreter. In fact she was probably the leading interpreter for Gosconcert, the organizers of all our tours. I knew, of course, that it was her duty to report every little thing to her superiors, which made me wonder if I really should have asked her about Boris. But I was sure Natasha was fond of me and was unlikely to report absolutely everything to her boss.

We certainly had a very strange chat about Boris: 'Yes,' said Natasha, 'I know him all right. But he's OK: you have nothing to fear from that direction. He's a gypsy and gypsies are very fond of music. Boris has a lovely voice himself, so perhaps that's his reason for getting in touch with you. He's safe enough. He also has some very influential friends, one in particular, but I'll leave you to find that out for yourself. It's way out of my class. But one small warning – don't believe everything he tells you. Remember he's a gypsy and telling stories comes as naturally to him as making love!' With that Natasha gave a sort of I've-got-a-secret smile and changed the subject.

The next night – the night I was to meet Boris – turned out to be very special. I spotted Tamara Khanum, one of the Russian 'greats', sitting in the front row. She was dressed in Uzbek national costume and her little hat was covered with a multitude of precious stones. Tamara Khanum was born in Armenia and soon became a National Artist of the Republic of Uzbekistan. She was worshipped like a goddess by all Uzbeks, but she was also an international artiste of great renown. In the years between the two world wars she had travelled with the Uzbek National Dance Ensemble all over the world. In Britain the Queen (now the Queen Mother) presented her with a gold medal, which is on display in the Uzbek National Museum in Tashkent. She was a super-talented, multi-lingual performer who had entertained the troops despite appalling conditions throughout World War Two, and had been made a National Artist of the USSR.

You can imagine that her presence at the concert caused great excitement among the audience. And not only the audience. Backstage word flew round. I looked at her through my spy hole. She had aged a lot, but it was thirty years since I had last seen her. I had fallen in love with her then and was thrilled to see her once again. It gave me an idea.

As soon as the finale of the first half drew near I moved out on stage as usual to join Robert in a number which I had written specially for him. It was called 'No More Tears' and was very much in the Russian style – a happy rhythmic song for the audience to clap to – but this time I waved the orchestra to silence. There was a great hush and Robert looked puzzled. I signalled to him not to worry and turned back to the audience. 'Friends,' I said, 'we are very privileged tonight. A great lady has honoured us with her presence. I give you – Tamara Khanum!' The full white spotlight picked out Tamara and the audience rose and exploded into applause.

Then, with what I hoped was impeccable timing, I went down from the stage to her seat and, kissing both her hands, thanked her for coming to the concert. Her reply was to kiss me on both cheeks, the Russian way. But the audience wouldn't stop clapping and cheering! She whispered to me, 'Repeat the song. Please . . .' and I returned to the stage, thinking that Tamara wanted to hear the interrupted song in full. But as soon as we started to play, Tamara Khanum stood up and made her way on to the stage. As she stepped on stage there was the deepest silence. She came forward and, taking each of us by the hand, led us into a dance in her Russo-Asian style.

We did our best to keep up with her, but the audience didn't care about our dancing. Flowers showered on to the stage and they were all for her. She gave a wonderful spontaneous performance and I don't think the Russian audience had ever seen anything quite like it.

And out of the corner of my eye I saw Boris, applauding and cheering and practically standing on his seat.

It took me a long time to get out of the building after the show. Robert had surpassed himself and the curtain calls seemed to go on for ever. But Boris had waited. He was alone. There was no sign of Maya. As he led me to his car – the Mercedes again – he said, 'I prefer to meet you by myself. It means we can talk more freely. We'll go to the "Veteo" – it's for members only and we can relax there. You won't be bothered by your fans!'

This time Boris's clothing was not quite so flamboyant but on his shirt collar there was still a flashing display of gems and he wore a well-tailored safari suit.

He also wore a thick gold bracelet and a Patek Philippe gold watch.

The 'Veteo' restaurant was controlled by the Russian artists' organization, and it was obvious as soon as we entered that everyone knew Boris. In fact most of the clients seemed to be competing with each other in the warmth of their greetings. We were shown to a table loaded with delicacies, including four different kinds of caviar, smoked fish, and good French wine in ice buckets. Such food was not available even in the best restaurants in Moscow. I must have looked impressed, for Boris said in a studied casual way, 'I asked them to put wine on ice, instead of that dreadful artificial Soviet champagne. You know the stuff – it's like coloured soda water!' I said nothing.

For the next few minutes we indulged in the usual opening remarks, broken only when Boris waved languidly – a definite keep-away-don't-you-dare-join-us kind of wave – to one or two women at nearby tables. Then he pulled his chair closer to mine and dropped his voice to a confidential level. 'You know, we gypsies have an inborn instinct about people. Directly I saw you I knew that you were the man I have been waiting for – the man I've been praying for. I knew I'd meet you one day.' Anyone overhearing his words might have thought we were a couple of gays dining together for the first time.

One thing was clear: Boris loved a touch of drama. 'I shall not tell you all today. I'd rather leave it to our next meeting in my flat. It won't be so crowded there, and anyway . . .' he glanced round ominously, 'who knows who's watching us this very minute!'

By then I was quite alarmed and a voice inside told me to put a stop to all this. I wanted to look straight into those green eyes and tell him that whatever it was he wanted to tell me didn't interest me at all. That I was only in Russia for one reason: to give concerts. That I was just a guest from Great Britain and didn't want to get involved in things that didn't concern me. But I didn't. Instead I remembered Natasha's voice saying, 'You have nothing to fear from that direction,' and kept quiet.

It was clear that Boris mistook my silence for assent. Once again he told me he was the son of a gypsy princess and that his mother had left him a great deal of money. 'I will show you some of my treasures when you visit me tomorrow. Come for lunch and you'll see for yourself.' It was obvious that Boris was holding back with difficulty. I felt that at any moment his restraint might snap and he would blurt it all out. That there was something important to blurt out, I had no doubt. He was relying on my curiosity to make me agree to go to his flat. And he was succeeding.

I then asked him where Maya was. 'To be honest,' said Boris, 'I took her to the theatre for companionship only. She's really a bit of a bore and also, one might say, bad medicine. She's Jewish and all she's looking for is someone from abroad to marry her and get her out of here. She has a lot of jewellery and very wealthy relatives in the United States, but her chances of getting out are very slim. Her late husband was a highly decorated captain of the KGB, so I don't think they'd let her go – just in case he talked in his sleep!'

That sort of talk made me even more nervous. Why was Boris, who hardly knew me, speaking so openly about such things? Was he a plant? Was I supposed to offer Maya the chance of escape? I decided that I would never repeat anything Boris told me. I realized too that by taking such a decision I had agreed to see Boris again.

THREE

I slept deeply that night and awoke late in the morning with a headache. Perhaps the wine at the restaurant hadn't been born in France after all – though it had tasted all right – or perhaps some of the fish had upset me. Either way, I felt distinctly under the weather. I remembered only too clearly that Boris was going to fetch me at 1 p.m. I hoped that Natasha would need me for some official function and that I could leave a message for Boris saying that I had forgotten some important business and was sorry. It was a vain hope.

Boris was waiting outside the hotel promptly at one o'clock. I wondered for a moment why he did not come in and wait in the foyer, but had little time to think about it as he drove us briskly through the busy streets of Moscow. Some of the militiamen controlling the traffic saluted Boris as we passed. What sort of man got such royal treatment – and in Moscow of all places? I thought for a moment that perhaps those who saluted were gypsies too, but that was an absurd explanation.

I didn't have much time to ponder further. We entered the driveway of a tall modern building and pulled up at the front entrance. 'Here we are,' said Boris. He got out and to my surprise took off the windscreen wipers and threw them inside the car before locking it carefully. 'In Moscow you've got to hide everything that can be removed – otherwise it's gone as soon as you turn your back!' Now I understood why

Boris had waited in the street outside the hotel near his car for me to come out. And now I understand why his flash car had no wing or door mirrors.

Inside, in the hall, sat the usual grim-faced guardian, just like the ones who grace the corridors of every hotel. She forced a grin which looked more like the snarl of an animal about to pounce. Boris told me later that the woman was there only to report the comings and goings of the high-ranking officials and media stars who had flats in the block. The thought of her reporting my visit merely added to the worries I already had about meeting Boris.

We entered the flat and I gazed around in amazement. I had stepped into a miniature museum. There were old paintings on the walls and Persian rugs on the floor. The splendid antique furniture was covered with bowls of the finest porcelain, icons and crystal vases. It was wealth of a kind that is never seen in Russia except in the state museums. For an individual to own such things told me more about Boris's power than any salutes from traffic police.

Evidently pleased with my reaction to his treasures, Boris asked what I would like to drink before lunch. 'I have some champagne on ice if you'd like that – the real stuff from France.' He filled our glasses – the correct flute shape and worth a fortune in themselves – and sat down in an armchair that looked as if it might have belonged to one of the Tsars. 'Let's drink to something,' he said. 'How about to life and all that comes with it?'

'I'll drink to that,' I said. Life certainly seemed good to Boris; as I looked round the room at all the treasures, he jumped up. 'Come on, you haven't seen half of it yet!'

There were three large rooms, each decorated in a different style. The bedroom had as its centrepiece an enormous four-poster bed. It was undoubtedly old but all the gold leaf glistened as though it had just been applied. Two luxurious bathrooms opened off the bedroom, and the kitchen at the other end of the flat contained all the latest labour-saving devices.

What had Boris done for Russia to deserve such wealth? The question loomed so large in my mind that I almost expected Boris to answer it without my having to put it into words. But there was no opportunity for questions; Boris was like a little boy showing off his toys.

'Look at this,' he said, opening yet another door to reveal a room stacked with hundreds of tins of food of British, American and German makes, interspersed with jars of coffee and bottles of every conceivable drink. Enough to feed the Kremlin for weeks, I thought. There were rails on the far side of the room from which hung masses of clothing of all kinds: suits and trousers for men and then rows of women's dresses, blouses, skirts and sheepskin coats. The sight of all this affluence obviously excited Boris. 'Anything you want, you can find here, my friend. This is how a real gypsy prince provides for himself and the people near him!' I felt very close to being bribed. But for what I didn't know.

Boris had not finished. He led me to another room and opened the huge drawers of an antique dresser. 'Look,' he boasted, 'some of these things came from the dining room of the Tsars!' I have no doubt he was telling the truth. There were whole dinner services of the most magnificent silver, all antique. 'Only the best, my friend,' beamed Boris, 'and, as you can see, Fabergé too.' I began to think I was dreaming.

The *pièce de résistance* was a sackful of jewellery which he emptied on the table between us. There were bracelets and rings and pendants, and loose gems too: diamonds, rubies, sapphires and emeralds winked in the light against a background of worked gold and old silver. I was speechless, Boris's green eyes, matching the emeralds, looked at me from behind the pile of jewels.

We walked back to our champagne in silence. I sensed that Boris was going to tell me now what he wanted from me. I sensed, too, my own folly in remaining even in the same room with him. But curiosity fought with fear and I wanted to hear his explanation of all this wealth. Boris sipped his champagne and started slowly: 'I told you, didn't I, that my mother was a gypsy princess . . . she left me a lot . . . and part of what you have seen was hers and part her mother's. And some must have come from even older times when the gypsies ran wild and free across the steppes and no doubt stole some of the trinkets you saw just now. But much of what you see is mine. It is priceless, and I got it for myself.' Boris paused there for a moment, drank some more, and seemed to be in two minds whether to go on. But in a moment he continued in the same low voice. 'Listen to me carefully. What I am going to tell you I have never told anyone before . . . if I had I wouldn't be here. But the truth is that I would gladly give everything that I possess – yes, all the things you have seen and more – for a passage to the West. Do you understand?'

His words shook me. Not just because what he had said was unexpected, but because it was too dangerous to listen to. I quickly interrupted him. 'Boris, you're not serious! You don't mean it and you shouldn't say it!'

'Oh yes, I mean it. I dream about it all the time. Freedom is more than wealth. You can't feel as I do because you live in the free world.'

I interrupted him again. 'From what I have seen, you are free. You seem to do what you want, go where you please and on top of that you have all this!'

'Free?' His voice took on a sombre note. 'You're like everyone else who is really free. You don't understand what it's like to be here. All this money gives me only limited freedom, and you can't feel free if you are wondering all the time how much longer it will last!'

He seemed to be in agony as he spoke. I tried to say

something, but he brushed it aside with a torrent of words. 'Do you know I feel like the King of Beggars who became the King of France for seven days only. For all this make-believe I am paying dearly, and maybe in the end I shall pay for it with my life! Do you understand now? As I told you when we first met, you are the man I have been waiting for. The man who can make my dreams come true. You are the man who can give me freedom – if you will. Free? Here? You're joking! . . . All right, I'll tell you my secret. Then you'll see how slender is the string on which my freedom hangs. The truth, my friend, is that I am the favourite lover of Brezhnev's daughter, Galina, and I will survive only as long as I continue to please her. All right, go on . . . what would you call me in the West? A gigolo? Yes, I'm good in bed but I fuck her for one reason only – to stay alive!'

He paused as if to gauge my reaction, but I gave none.

'Of course it wasn't like that in the beginning. In the beginning I thought I loved her, or maybe it was just the thrill of fucking the daughter of the most powerful man in the world. Whatever it was, we enjoyed each other. And she knows how to please a man . . . well, she should. Her lovers come from all walks of life – ballet dancers, writers, film directors – and she's not averse to taking anyone who strikes her fancy, even off the streets. She can't help it, you know: if she hears a man has a big prick she's got to have it. She's married, but it makes no difference. Her husband is a big shot in the Ministry of Internal Affairs. That's the standing joke in Moscow . . . that she's really the Minister for Internal Affairs! But he's away most of the time, out of Moscow. Anyway, I'm her favourite lover, no doubt about that. But it's an exhausting business, I can tell you . . . the lady is very, very demanding. And you call that freedom!'

I now understood what Natasha had meant when she

said Boris had powerful friends and one in particular. As a result, I could do little justice to the excellent lunch which was prepared and served by a handsome woman who appeared from nowhere and who was introduced by Boris as his housekeeper.

I toyed with the food in silence. Boris too was quiet, shooting occasional glances at me from under his long feminine eyelashes. I reflected that if I were to tell anybody about my experiences that day, I would not be believed. I thought I knew Russia well. I had seen it in war and in peace but I had never imagined anything like this was possible in this strictly controlled and heavily policed country. How could someone like Boris circulate freely and flaunt his wealth against the familiar Russian background of grim and fearful everyday life? Surely the KGB wouldn't tolerate it? How powerful Old Man Brezhnev must be if his daughter could openly consort with this gypsy! Now I realized why the militia on point duty saluted him. Better safe than sorry – after all Galina might be with him in the car! But what did he mean when he said that I was the man he had been waiting for? Surely he understood that I was not going to put my head in a KGB noose for him?

Once again it seemed that Boris had read my thoughts. 'Let me explain. I know all about you. I know about your war experiences. I know about your stardom here during the war. Important people here respect you and feel it is quite safe to let you walk the streets of Russia. In other words they have decided you are OK. So they will not suspect you as readily as they would anyone else . . .'

I didn't like the sound of this at all. 'Suspect me? Suspect me of what? I am certainly not going to do anything against the law – you can be sure of that! In fact I don't like the way this conversation is going one little bit. I think I'd better leave!' I projected my voice on these last words towards the door. If the woman who served lunch was not Boris's mistress, then she was most certainly installed with him to report all goings-on to the KGB. I wanted to make sure she got the record straight.

'Don't be silly, I'm not going to ask you to do anything against the law. I'm not stupid. But I must get away and you can help me.'

'How?' I spoke the words as though the idea was a failure even before I heard it.

'I have a plan,' he said, almost airily, 'but there's no hurry. I'll tell you more about it next time we meet.'

'No you won't, because we won't be meeting again. I'm not going to let down the people who have trusted me. I'm staying neutral and I'm minding my own business. Understand?'

'Of course, of course, I understand your feelings entirely. And to show you that I do, I'll tell you my plan and then you'll see that there's no danger for you in it at all.'

I tried to protest. I could almost feel the presence of the woman outside the door. Don't be a fool, Boris, I thought, she'll report you right away. I pulled a face and nodded towards the door. Boris looked at me in surprise.

'You can't think . . .! Yes, you do. You must take me for a fool. Do you really think I would speak so freely if I had one of those human KGB recorders in the flat? That woman is one of my family, a gypsy like me. She would never rat on me. She also happens to be a deaf mute!' Boris grinned from ear to ear and managed for a moment to look ugly and menacing. But the grin faded and his good looks returned.

'I'll tell you what, Maestro, how would you like to be a very rich man? I can make you one – after what you have seen you can have no doubt of that. Think about it. I can get something smuggled out for you – no risk for you – which you can sell in the West and retire on the proceeds. How about that?'

Simple avarice made me listen.

'For a man like you, it would be nothing. Something you could do whenever you had a spare moment . . . All I really want you to do is to teach me how to use my voice to sing popular songs. I want to learn how to phrase and project my voice from a stage. I don't mean heavy operatic songs. Will you teach me a few of your skills?'

At last I saw what Boris was up to, though it took me several moments to grasp the full implications. Boris's plan was to learn to sing popular songs so that with his fine voice he could join some folk group or ensemble and . . . and then supposing they were to go on a foreign tour! On the face of it it was clever, though it did cross my mind at the time that Boris was underestimating both the KGB and Galina Brezhnev. But that was his problem.

The important thing was that I didn't have to risk anything to help him with this first stage. But even so I started to protest, saying that we were off on tour in a couple of days' time and, though I would have liked to help him, it would be impossible. I underestimated Boris to the extent of thinking that he hadn't taken this into account.

First he appealed to the worst side of human nature: he opened a box and took out a big diamond ring which flashed in the light. 'This is a very old and beautiful ring . . . it used to be my mother's. It's about two carats and not a flaw in it. How about taking this as an advance for my lessons?'

I said no, and meant it.

'Look,' he said, 'you take the ring. You have nothing to fear. It really was my mother's and I give it to you. All I want is a few singing lessons. What's the harm in that? I swear you won't be involved in anything else.'

I thought immediately of the old saying 'beware of a gypsy when he swears', but he stuffed the ring into the top pocket of my jacket. I promised myself that I would teach him to sing but nothing more.

'And don't worry about the tour,' he added, 'it's only fair that I should come to you. I'll join you wherever you are. I'll bring my pianist and all you have to do is spare a fraction of your valuable time . . .' The deal was done.

When Boris dropped me back at the hotel, I was full of that sense of doom which you usually associate only with a huge hangover. But this depression didn't come from Boris's champagne, it came from the realization that I had been a complete and utter fool. I had done exactly what I had cautioned so many people on our tours not to do. I had become involved – even if only in a minor way – in a plot against the state.

The fact that my part in Boris's attempt to defect was hardly likely to escape notice made me very frightened. I suspected, despite Boris's confidence, that our meetings had already been noted. Just thinking about it made me shiver, and my experience of Russia told me that Boris wouldn't get away with it. Gypsies are not accepted as true Russians. Although they are sometimes rated highly as entertainers by the Russian élite, the ordinary Russian doesn't find them entertaining and regards them very differently: as con-men and thieves. In their role as entertainers they sometimes receive medals from the state; for their other pursuits they usually end up in the labour camps.

It was also very hard for me to believe that the daughter of the Supreme Head of the Soviet Union would associate with a gypsy, let alone take one as a lover. If what Boris had told me was true, then Galina Brezhnev's sexual aberrations could not possibly have escaped the notice of the Soviet hierarchy, who are ever on guard against any disturbance of their secret lifestyle, their dachas and their luxuries. So how could such a liaison be allowed?

As we left Moscow and started our tour I was a worried man. I became even more worried when, after a few days at Vilnyus, our first stop in Lithuania, Boris arrived. As promised, he had brought his own pianist with him and there was nothing for me to do but to get on with it. The lessons were not difficult. Boris was talented and I could see that he would turn into a good pop singer without too much trouble. He had brought a tape-recorder with him to record everything I taught him. This, he said, was so that he could practise without me after I left Russia.

Once during a lesson Boris threw his coat on to a chair. A cascade of jewellery fell out of the pockets and rolled on the floor. He didn't even bother to stop singing and left it lying there until the lesson was over. I felt a sudden chill. Where had he got it from? Why was he carrying it? The questions remained with me, unanswered, until I climbed gratefully aboard a jet on my way home to England.

FOUR

It was spring when I next flew into Moscow. In the taxi from the airport to the Metropole, though snow still survived in hard-packed heaps, it was impossible not to thrill to its approach. Winter was on the retreat and I felt happy to be back.

The feeling didn't last long. I was in the middle of unpacking when the phone rang. It was Boris. He gave me a warm welcome but when he proceeded to set out all the things he had arranged for me during my stay in Moscow my heart really sank.

I had come to Russia on my own this time, in order to catch a very big fish. I wanted to arrange a visit of the composer, Aram Khatchaturian, to London where he would conduct the London Symphony Orchestra in concerts of his music. I also hoped he would record for EMI. It was not going to be easy to persuade the maestro to come to London and the last thing I wanted was Boris taking up my precious time with things that he wanted me to do. My light-hearted mood had gone and in its place was a big depression called Boris.

I started to tell him that what he had in mind was quite impossible and that I doubted if I would have time to see him on this trip, but I ended up agreeing to discuss matters over dinner that night. I don't quite know how I let him talk me into it. There was something about him that I found very difficult to resist. I had determined in London to tell him if he contacted me that I was not prepared to continue with his lessons. And yet here I was having dinner with him on my first night in Moscow.

In the meantime I tried to put Boris out of my mind and concentrate on my pursuit of Khatchaturian. I knew it was not going to be easy even though I had the blessing of the Soviet authorities: Khatchaturian was so important to Russia that no one gave him orders. It was he who decided what he would or wouldn't do and I knew he would be difficult to persuade. And if he once set against the idea, no one would move him. I finished putting away my things.

Boris called for me at 7 p.m., whisked me past the hotel restaurant and out through the front door. He was smartly dressed as usual and we exchanged pleasantries as we pushed our way through the crowd on the pavement. It was some seconds before I realized why there was a crowd there. They were all standing around a brand-new Pontiac which turned out to belong to Boris. It was clear that he had not changed his flamboyant habits, and was still asking for trouble.

He drove skilfully through the early-evening traffic and the car bounced over the patches of poor surface until we arrived outside the Writers' Club. He parked just outside, but once again he took the precaution of locking the windscreen wipers inside the car.

I had heard of the Writers' Club, but had never been there. By Russian standards its restaurant is very exclusive and the food and drink of a much better quality than in most other places. The clientele is well-spoken, well-dressed and includes members of the Nomenclatura, the Soviet ruling élite.

I felt I was among them when Boris introduced me to the people at our table. It was clear that they had been drinking heavily while they waited for us. There was a general, whose flashy uniform was almost hidden by clusters of medals; the director of a drama theatre; the director of the state circus, and a producer of the

Moscow Music Hall Ensemble. I was among the privileged few of Soviet society.

The conversation during the meal was mainly 'vodka talk', lots of words meaning very little. It was entertaining enough, until the general started trying to pick an argument with me. He was drunk and started boasting about how mighty was the undefeated Red Army which, he assured me, wanted only peace with the West. There was no point in getting involved in another war, was there? 'After all, we Russians won the last one single-handed!' Perhaps it was to provoke me, or perhaps he really believed it – but I wouldn't be drawn.

He was starting to get really nasty when the producer of the music hall smoothed things over by telling me how elegant and polished he found the British performers. 'We have a lot of talented artistes in Russia,' he said, 'but we are still well behind the English. We'd like to learn from them. I wonder if you would agree to meet me later and talk about things?'

'With pleasure,' I said. 'Perhaps you'd ring me and we could arrange it . . .'

Suddenly Boris interrupted, 'Gentlemen, I'm sorry but we must go now. The maestro has so much to do during his stay in Moscow . . .' And taking my arm, he led me off to collect our coats.

Once outside the club, I thought that Boris would go straight to his car, but he steered me to the left towards the embankment of the Moskva river. A little way along Nabereznaya Street we sat down on a bench and inhaled the cool air. Boris started to apologize: 'I hope you'll excuse those idiots at our table!'

'Of course,' I said, nearly as frosty as the air. 'They weren't so bad. In fact I quite liked your friend from the music hall – he seemed very enthusiastic and quite devoted to his work . . .'

Angered by my attitude, Boris tore into the man: 'You think so? He has never created anything of his own. All he does is copy other people – from the West, from the provinces, from everywhere. And he doesn't even copy things well. When he takes something from the West and then presents it here, it's a bad caricature of the real thing . . . and don't bother to disagree with me. I know what I'm talking about. Gypsy Boris knows a lot of things. That is why I want out. And the sooner the better!'

Here he goes again, I thought wearily.

'Take that look off your face,' said Boris, 'and listen to me. I'm not like one of those morons in the club!'

There was something in his words – a note, an inflection, the shading of a phrase – which struck a chord in me. It was something only a man who has known fear can scent. I suddenly sensed that Boris too was afraid. The moment had no sooner come than it had gone, but I had heard it.

'Things have changed. Why look surprised? Why be surprised? Things change in Russia just as in the West. They change all the time. No one's situation is ever permanent. You can climb nearly to the top and then have a sudden fall . . .'

I didn't like the sound of this at all, but Boris was in full flow. 'When I first met you, I asked for a simple favour. I asked you to teach me to sing popular songs and you didn't refuse. I'm grateful for what you did. But it's not going to work. I have to change my plans and try something else.'

'Why won't it work? What's happened?'

'Galina found out somehow,' said Boris matter-of-factly. 'I don't know quite how, but she knew . . .'

And if Galina knew, I thought, with my heart in my throat, then the KGB knew too.

'She's a bitch! She let me know by little clues, nothing outright, just hints. Once, just as I thought she was having her orgasm, I suddenly realized she was laughing. Laughing! And then she sniggered, "Who's the big strong pop singer, then?" and she slid off and grabbed me so hard that I thought she was going to snap my cock off.'

'Who told her?' My heart raced.

'Who told her?!' repeated Boris in amazement. 'Don't be so bloody stupid. She's a bitch, a possessive bitch. I'm just one of her lapdogs and if one of them has been naughty she finds out soon enough. I was mad to think that she wouldn't put two and two together on this one. Who told her? Who do you think! Who tells her everything? Just look across the river . . .'

I did as I was told.

'Don't make it so bloody obvious! You see the house opposite us with the blinds drawn on the second floor? I'm willing to bet we are being photographed through those blinds at this very moment. The bloody KGB are everywhere.'

Fear made me angry: 'You're big trouble and I want no part in it!' I got up and set off down the street. Boris jumped in front of me and, walking backwards, tried to charm me out of my rage. In the sharp cold of the air I could smell his after-shave. Like most things about him, it had come from the West.

'Look, you're not involved. Galina will think you didn't know what you were doing. She probably doesn't even know that you exist . . .'

'You can't expect me to believe that! I don't want any part of this. I'm going back to the hotel now and that's that!'

Boris stopped. Which meant I had to stop too. We were right under a street light and it picked out his features unkindly. His nose had a slight hook to it. Now in the light of the lamp it looked heavily hooked, almost a beak. But the light improved his eyes, which sparkled a grey-green. His teeth in comparison looked yellow, bared in that infectious smile which I already knew he could switch on and off at will. He put out a hand to stop my bumping into him and the little black 'handbag' nearly clipped me on the chin.

'Please don't be angry, I'm in enough trouble as it is. Let's go back to the car and I'll drive you to the hotel if that's what you want.'

He said it in a little-boy-lost way, turning the smile down at the same time. Suddenly I knew he was a homosexual. It came as a shock, especially after all his talk of sexual acrobatics with Galina, but there was no doubt in my mind. This sudden realization made it hard to concentrate on what Boris was saying, but when I heard him mention the KGB again I forced myself to listen. He was saying that Galina Brezhnev probably found out from several people. There was the woman 'keeper' at his block of flats for example. 'I feed her a lot of duff information,' said Boris, 'but she will certainly have reported that you had lunch with me. Then the theatre director at Vilnyus will have reported that you were giving me lessons . . . and then dear Gala – she's very bright, you know – will have put two and two together. She looks on this as a game. She plays games both in and out of bed, does Gala . . .'

Boris had now taken me by the arm and was steering me towards the car. I no longer minded – it would have been difficult to find transport at that time of night anyway. I told myself I would let him drive me to the hotel and then I would be finished with him for ever.

He talked on as we walked: 'I'm lucky that Gala enjoys her games, though sometimes they become quite exhausting. At the moment I'm the best piece in her games box. She wants me – too often I can tell you – so she doesn't ask Daddy to arrange for me to disappear. But I'm quite aware that she could do so at any moment and Daddy would just sweep me off the board.

'And there's another reason why Gala keeps moving me around the board in her games: she hates her husband! Oh yes, she really hates him. He's in the game too. She uses me to humiliate him. A man in his position could have me sent to a labour camp, but he daren't do that in case Gala tells Daddy that Yuri

Churbanov is getting above himself and that he has hurt her. Not even the fact that he is a minister would save him then. So you see what deadly games our Gala plays!'

I was listening. Listening hard. Boris was lifting the lid all right. And I needed to know who was who in the stew he revealed.

'You've got nothing to fear!' Boris spoke with something close to contempt. 'You've been thoroughly checked, you can be sure about that. I don't have to tell you that, do I? You're a clever man, Stanley, you know how to mind your own business and that's good enough for the KGB.'

I wish I had been clever enough to do just that, I thought. I should have minded my own business. And, whatever Boris said, it was odds-on the KGB knew I hadn't.

'It isn't only this damn country I want to escape from, but Galina Brezhnev. She's bloody clever. Do you know what she's done now?' It wasn't really a question. 'Galina Brezhnev is more powerful than the KGB, the Politburo and all the rest of them put together. Yes, I mean it. You know what she's done . . . ? She's got me into the Bolshoi, she's got me a permanent card as a singer. That membership means that it wouldn't be ethical for me to take part in light-entertainment singing. So she's clipped my wings. Now I have to obey all the stupid rules and regulations of the Bolshoi, and you can't imagine how strict a great classical institution like that is.

'I thought perhaps I could fool her even so. The Bolshoi goes abroad, and perhaps I could wangle my way on to one of their trips. But by God she's clever . . . she knows that there are long queues to go on the overseas tours and naturally enough the first places go to the older members – I'll be a hundred before I qualify!' He sounded as if he was going to burst into tears.

'But I have other plans.' The echo of his voice made

me shiver. 'Perhaps you noticed I am well in with some important people? I know you think they are drunken bores and they did behave badly tonight, but they're powerful. The director of the Mkhat Theatre and the director of the Moscow Circus – they travel abroad. And I hear they make a fortune doing so. In fact it's rumoured that the circus director has huge sums in secret accounts abroad. He evidently takes bribes from artistes who want to travel abroad, but there are so many rumours about his money that nobody really knows. I don't like him, but I have to stay friendly with him. Who knows, I may need him in the future, though I doubt if he really has a future. I think his days are numbered.'

We had reached the car and as soon as I got in and Boris had gone through the ritual of replacing his windscreen wipers I asked him why he didn't give up the idea of escaping to the West and settle down. 'Even the KGB would leave you alone then.'

He looked at me in amazement. 'Settle down? Settle down! You haven't understood a word I've been saying! You have no idea what it's like for me, have you? Where do you suggest I "settle down" as you call it? She'll find me wherever I go in Russia. The KGB don't worry me so much as she does. She's selfish, corrupt and – make no mistake about it – she can be very, very vicious. She needs me. Do you understand that? She needs me. Needs me to play her rotten sex games. I was always quite normal before I met her, but now she's made me bisexual. She gets young boys into her bed and then gets drunk while watching me make love to them. Normal sex doesn't seem to turn her on any more – you wouldn't believe what I have to do to give her pleasure . . . And I'm trapped. She needs me, but I need her power and protection too.' He put his head in his hands.

'Without her, I'm finished. She's flaunted me so often in front of her husband that he'll make sure they get me in the end. It's only a matter of time before they pounce – so I've got to get out first. Let's change the subject,' he said suddenly and pulled away from the kerb.

As he did so, two drunks swayed right into our path. Boris swerved violently and just missed them. As their faces passed my window, I could see from their blank eyes that they were very close to collapse. In fact as I looked back they sagged to the ground in the middle of the road. 'All Russia is drunk,' said Boris, glancing in the rear mirror. 'It's the only real escape from all our miseries.'

Boris drove on past the Bolshoi up to Dzherzhinsky Square. As we passed the monument and he prepared to make the U-turn to get to the Metropole, the white-gloved hand of a militiaman made Boris screech to a halt.

'Your documents, please, Comrade.'

'I don't have them on me,' said Boris calmly, 'but I can assure you I have them at home.'

The man said nothing, but signalled to Boris to wait. He disappeared into his booth and came out with a screwdriver in his hand and began to unscrew the Pontiac's numberplates.

'What the hell are you doing?!' Boris was no longer calm; he sounded almost hysterical at this abuse of his precious car. When both numberplates were off, the militiaman came back to Boris's window and said, 'You understand that you are not permitted to drive in Moscow without numberplates. It is against the law. When you show me your documents, then I shall be able to return the plates to you.'

Boris resumed control and the tone was that of a sergeant-major talking to a humble recruit: 'Now listen to me. You put those plates back at once or you are going to regret the day you were born.'

'Oh yes?' he sneered. 'Do I understand you to be threatening me, Comrade? Come on, I like this. You're the one who's going to regret it. You think I'm afraid of guys like you, parading around in expensive foreign cars? Just who do you think you are?'

I laid a restraining hand on Boris's arm, but he shook it off. He got out of the car and told me to follow him. I hesitated and as I did so the militiaman tried to stop Boris, saying that he couldn't leave the car where it was but must drive it away to a proper parking spot. Boris pushed him aside. 'You do it, Comrade. Don't you know it's against the law to drive a car in Moscow without numberplates?'

I trailed along after Boris as he steamed towards the nearest public phonebox. I waited outside. Through the glass I could hear some muffled exchanges and as he put the phone down he began to smile.

By the time we got back to the Pontiac, there was another car beside it. It was a Chaika limousine and my heart sank because Chaikas are alloted only to high officials and it looked to me as if some big guns had been summoned to deal with Boris. But the militiaman looked far from happy. A man in civilian clothes was standing in front of him gesticulating angrily and ordering him to return the numberplates to Comrade Buryatsa. Boris grinned at the militiaman's discomfort as he went sheepishly back to his booth and came out with the plates. He held them out to Boris, but Boris kept his hands by his sides. 'You took them off, Comrade, you put them back.'

After we were on our way again, Boris anticipated my question and said simply. 'I rang Galina. Do you believe me now?'

'I do,' I said. And I did. 'But why do you go out of your way to provoke people? You act as though you want to be destroyed. And yet at the same time you say you want out. It doesn't make sense.'

'It may not to you,' said Boris, 'but it does to me. OK, so one plan has failed. I'll have to try something else, that's all. I'll go on until I get a break. But it doesn't mean I've got to suffer fools gladly in between. That would be asking too much of a gypsy!' He grinned and again that wolfish look came over his face. 'And, after all, I've got some insurance . . .'

'Insurance? How can you be insured against the KGB?'

'KGB . . . you've got the KGB on the brain. I tell you, I've got insurance – even against them. I'll tell you some other time. One thing is sure – if I go, I'll take a lot of others with me.'

FIVE

I like the old Metropole Hotel. I first stayed there at the beginning of the war, just before the Molotov–Ribbentrop pact exploded in Stalin's face and Hitler attacked Russia. I remembered so many things each time I walked through the front door: the restaurant with the flags of different nations on the tables, the shining dancefloor around a beautiful fountain, the discreet music from a small light orchestra. I lamented the 'grand hotel' atmosphere as I took the lift to the third floor.

As I headed for my room the *dezhurnaya* handed me a slip of paper. The writing on it was in English and she told me it had been left by an 'English lady'. As soon as I read the message I knew that my visitor had been no English lady but the very Russian Irena, wife of one of the leading actors in the Soviet Union. Irena, too, was obviously a good enough actress to convince my *dezhurnaya* that I had been visited by a foreigner.

As soon as I was in my room I dialled the number on the paper. Irena answered. 'You naughty man! Why didn't you tell us you were back in Moscow? No, no excuses. We are very upset!'

I told her I was on a delicate mission.

'I know,' said Irena, 'in fact I know everything about your visit. As soon as I heard, Andrei and I decided to offer you our help. Believe me you will need it!'

'What do you mean?' I asked, really to staunch Irena's

flow. It was not for nothing that she was known as the 'walking, talking Moscow newspaper'. Even so she took me by surprise.

'Your meeting with Aram Khatchaturian tomorrow. We know he has a weakness for pretty women – so I am going to come with you and act as your secretary!'

I tried to explain that there was no need for her to come. The meeting had been arranged by the Gosconcert office and was really only routine. She cut in again, her voice full of sarcasm: 'How refreshing to listen to someone so romantic and naïve . . . My dear, you have been away too long and you obviously don't know Khatchaturian at all. He is not an easy man – in fact he is very difficult. To start with he's an Armenian and you know what they say: an Armenian can sell ten Jews and twenty Arabs before breakfast! No, I'm coming with you tomorrow. I'll pick you up at 9.45. After all, it's not far from the hotel to the Academy of Music – that is where you're meeting him, isn't it?' She didn't wait for my reply.

I sat for a moment with the receiver still in my hand. How could she have known all these details? Perhaps Boris had told her? He had told me he knew her when he was trying to impress me over dinner the previous night. Well, so what? It didn't really matter.

It was starting to get dark and I walked to the window to draw the curtains. I could still see the street below: people moved along in a dark mass; nothing had really changed. It was over thirty years since my first visit and I could have been looking at the same scene. Western faces don't really fit here, I thought. I pictured Boris again in my mind and thought that he didn't fit either. I shivered and went to run a bath.

After my bath I debated whether to have some food sent up or to go down to the restaurant. I chose the restaurant but nearly turned back at the doors: the room was packed and the noise of the music only just bearable. But Sasha, my favourite waiter, spotted me and found me a table straight away.

As I ate my meal the music seemed to get louder and louder, but it didn't worry the couples on the dance-floor. They weren't really dancing, just gesticulating at each other. I thought how little grace they had and how different it had all been in the old days . . .

'Good evening, Maestro.' The greeting brought me back to reality. The restaurant manager stood at my table. He was a tall, handsome man and could not have been more than fifty although his hair was completely grey. I remembered him from the old days when he had been a young apprentice waiter at the Metropole. After the formalities about whether I had enjoyed my meal, he asked me if I would join him for a private drink in his office. It was an unusual request, but I followed him. I sat down in the chair he indicated and he carefully closed the door.

He poured out two glasses of a very good vodka and raised his in a toast to me. I wondered what the real point of it all was and I didn't have to wait long to find out. Almost at once he launched into one of those flattering Russian speeches which take a very long time to get to the point. 'Maestro, we've known each other for a long time now and you must be aware of how much I respect you for everything you did for our people during the war – your songs and your music were an inspiration. They have become part of our folklore. Many people here consider you part of our history . . .'

He finally got to the point: '. . . which is why I consider it my duty to tell you – straight from the heart and as a friend – that you should be more careful about the company you keep . . .'

'What do you mean?' I tried to stay calm.

He rushed on as though trying to get it over with: 'Some of the individuals I have seen you with are not appropriate company.'

'The people you have seen me with here are state

officials who are connected with my business. Or they are stars of the Bolshoi, of films, or television. What do you mean, not appropriate company!'

'No, no, no! I am not referring to them!' He sounded almost hysterical at the idea that he was denouncing Party dignitaries. It was abundantly clear that he had Boris in mind, but I pretended not to understand. And then, as though it had suddenly dawned on me: 'You can't mean, surely, no . . . you know with whom . . .?' I had not intended to complete the sentence, but the manager cut in swiftly. 'Yes, yes, I know . . . but it is my duty to advise you against . . . you understand?'

I understood only too well. It was no surprise that the manager should be working for the KGB; if he hadn't, he would never have reached the top ranks of the Metropole staff. Had he reported on me all those years ago when we first met? I wondered whether this was an official warning about Boris – or was the Metropole manager exceeding his duties and giving me a friendly warning of his own? Either way the message was clear. I thanked him and assured him that I would be on my guard from now on. I didn't assure him that I wouldn't see Boris again because in some strange way the warning did nothing but increase my interest in Gypsy Boris.

Irena and I arrived outside the academy fifteen minutes early. Irena switched off the engine and proceeded to fill me in on all the latest goings-on in Moscow society, who was married to whom and who wasn't, who got the best film parts and why, who was in gaol and who wasn't but should have been. Suddenly she mentioned Boris. I looked carefully into her face to see if she too had been put up to warning me off, but I could see no sign.

'I always thought gypsies were clever and cunning people, but now I'm not so sure. Boris is neither of these things. Perhaps he's not a gypsy after all.'

'Why do you say that?'

'Oh, I don't know – probably because he makes me so angry. He parades and shows off so much. I tell you it's something we have never seen before in Moscow. God knows where he will end up!'

'Surely his influential friends will protect him?'

'Influential friends! They're just using him. Especially her.'

'Perhaps it's love.'

'Lust and selfishness, more like. She's rotten to the core, she is. I haven't got enough fingers to count the number of marriages she's destroyed, and as for the number of men . . . It seems nobody can resist the daughter of the Tsar!'

As she was saying this Irena switched on the car radio and turned the volume up full. She laughed at my look of surprise, but there was no humour in it. 'Sorry,' she said, 'force of habit. Maybe the car's bugged. Anything is possible in Moscow.'

The subject was dropped and we began to discuss my meeting with Khatchaturian. 'He can be very difficult. He has an enormous chip on his shoulder, possibly because he became famous only very late in life. He was born in a little village in Georgia of Armenian parents. You can imagine what a struggle he had in making his way to Moscow and breaking through into the ranks of the hierarchy. And even when he did he was never accorded the same sort of honours that went to Prokofiev and Shostakovitch, and I think he feels that deeply.'

I told Irena that his adagio from *Spartacus* had been a huge success in England and that it had been used as the theme music for one of British television's most popular series – *The Onedin Line* – which had first given me the idea of bringing him to London.

'It's a good idea, but Aram hasn't visited England for over twenty years, since he fell out with an impresario there, and from what I hear he is not on speaking terms with at least another forty impresarios all over the world. No wonder Gosconcert have left you to face the lion all by yourself.'

I looked at my watch. It was time. 'We'll see. Let's go and meet your lion.'

It wasn't as simple as that. As soon as I gave my name to the porter he handed me a slip of paper. The note was short: 'Cannot see you today. Busy chairing the exams' committee. Sorry.' It was signed Aram Illyitch. Disappointment mingled with anger – all that work and prepartion reduced to a rude little note.

Irena obviously felt the same way. 'Wait here,' she said to me, brushing the porter aside and running up the stairs. Two minutes later she reappeared at the top of the stairs, a broad smile on her face. 'It's all right. He'll see you.'

The bulky figure of Aram Khatchaturian sat at a desk in a small room. His age showed clearly, but his eyes were alive and alert. He made no effort to apologize but got straight down to business. I told him that London was ready to welcome him, that it had been twenty years since his last visit, and that he was bound to be a huge success.

'Success?' he said touchily. 'Success? I have all the success I need right here. And what is success anyway? It's like a hero's medal – you can't buy anything with it. Why should I bother with all that travelling and hard work when I end up with practically nothing?'

I tried to reassure him that the trip to London would be different, and Irena said firmly: 'Stanley won't let you down – my husband and I have known him for years. If you agree to go, you will be treated like royalty.'

'Better than that,' I cut in, 'you will be treated like Aram Illyitch Khatchaturian!'

To my relief he grinned, and after a long silence said, 'OK, I agree. Go ahead and make the arrangements.'

We shook hands on the deal, but my sense of triumph was tempered when he added, as if by way of an afterthought: 'I am not a healthy man. I have had three operations in a very short time and it is thanks to my family that I am still alive. I shall have to take my niece to London – she looks after me like a nurse – and my son and his wife . . .' His voice trailed off and I wondered briefly if he was thinking of adding any more relatives to the list. It was going to be impossible to budget for three extra people, but I had no choice. I heard myself say: 'No problem.'

The Gosconcert officials whom I went to see straight afterwards thought there was a very big problem. They could authorize him and his pianist, but not members of his family . . . and what about the cost? I suggested that they give me permission to have the concert in the Albert Hall filmed for television to help offset the overheads. 'Absolutely impossible. Completely out of our jurisdiction. Too many departments to go through . . .' Though I knew they were not being deliberately obstructive, I resolved not to be put off. If Khatchaturian's visit to London depended on his having his family with him, then somehow I had to find a way of arranging it.

That evening there was a party for Andrei's sixtieth birthday. I arrived a little early, but even so the party was in full swing and it was clear that the guests had already been through a dozen toasts or more. Irena had promised that a lot of interesting people would be there, and in a short space of time I was introduced to many famous names from the world of the arts.

I was just beginning to enjoy myself when Irena suddenly appeared with Boris. His entrance caused the buzz to die down. In the near-silence Irena said: 'He came to see you, Stanley.' Everyone stared and I hardly knew what to say. Finally I made a limp-wristed gesture and said in a camp voice, 'Really? How lovely, darling!' The joke was in bad taste, but everyone laughed, the awkward moment passed, and conversation rose again to its previous level.

'I had to see you.'

'What do you want?'

'Don't be like that. I want you to come to lunch tomorrow.'

'I'm busy.'

'You must come. Gala will never forgive me if you don't. She's dying to meet you.'

'Gala?' My resolution was already giving way.

'Don't pretend. Galina Brezhev of course. I've told her you'll be there.'

Irena returned to fill our glasses again, telling Boris he should drink to catch up on everyone else. The next time she filled his glass he took something out of his little bag and pressed it into her hand. It was a small, gold, enamelled brooch, obviously very old and worth a small fortune.

'Boris, you mustn't. Take it back.'

'No, it's for you. It will look wonderful on you. It's only a trifle – it used to be my mother's.' (Every piece of jewellery had evidently been his mother's.)

Irena tried reasoning with him: 'It's very kind of you, Boris, but it's not my birthday, it's Andrei's.'

It didn't work. 'I have something for him too.' He produced a gold five-rouble piece which he presented to Andrei. Once again the gift was no trinket. The coin was a collectors' item, rare and very valuable. Where did he get it all? It struck me as odd that he seemed to be able to have all the jewellery he wanted, yet he couldn't get abroad. Surely he could have bribed his way out? I determined to tackle him about it when he was sober.

The party progressed to the maudlin stage and when someone produced a guitar, Boris began to sing a gypsy song. He sang it beautifully and at one crescendo tears poured down his cheeks. Everyone applauded and cried out for more.

'Friends,' said Boris, 'I'm not going to apologize for my tears – they come from deep within my heart. I cry for the world that is gone, for the spirit of the old songs, for the days full of hope. I give you a toast: to the old days, the old songs, and above all . . . to hope!'

I wondered how many of those present knew of Boris's plans for the future. As we drank the toast, there was a loud ring on the doorbell.

SIX

Everyone stared at the tall man in the doorway. He had that well-fed fleshy look associated with over-indulgence. Yet he was clearly no playboy, but a man of authority. He looked round as though bewildered to find himself in the middle of someone else's party. As he did so, I felt Boris reach out and put something in my lap. I looked down, and saw Boris's black handbag.

The party atmosphere had drained away, and all eyes were on the stranger. It was Martha, a gypsy actress, who broke the silence: 'This is my friend Sasha. I asked him to give me a lift home . . . I had no idea it was so late!' Then it was Irena's turn. She spoke out like a good hostess but there was a formal ring to her invitation – 'Please . . . sit down . . . have a drink. We're celebrating my husband's birthday . . .' Her voice trailed off. The tension in the room was almost tangible.

The man raised his glass in a silent toast to Andrei and then turned almost immediately to me.

'And you, sir? Who are you bringing us this time?' If I hadn't known before that he was KGB, I knew now. I had never seen him before, yet he knew me and clearly knew about my business too.

I strung along: 'I don't know for sure,' I said, attempting a casual tone. 'A lot depends on the Ministry of Culture and Gosconcert.'

'You'll have no trouble there, I'm sure. You have a very good name with them.'

'I hope so.'

The conversation continued in a difficult, restrained way until Martha took the KGB man by the arm and suggested it was time to go. The party seemed to have lost its cohesion and very soon afterwards began to break up. Boris reclaimed his handbag and offered me a lift back to the hotel.

'Come on, let's have a little walk,' he said, stopping the car at Marx Prospect. It was a mild night and we set off at a gentle pace towards Red Square. When we reached the GUM department store, Boris looked round furtively for anyone who might overhear him before launching into his version of events at the party.

'That bastard didn't just come to fetch the gypsy girl: it was all carefully planned in advance. He was on duty, make no mistake about it, and checking up on us. That means someone higher up wants to know what we were up to. See how late he came – wanted to make sure we were all a bit drunk and our tongues were loosened. You don't have to worry – it was really me he was after . . . that's why I passed you the purse. He's been shadowing me for ages – I thought maybe he'd come for me at last!'

Boris suddenly stopped talking and pointed towards the Kremlin as though showing a tourist one of Moscow's sights. A moment later a militiaman passed us. When he was out of sight, Boris started up again. 'There are a number of KGB tailing me. I recognize quite a few faces every time I go out!'

'Haven't you told Galina?'

'Wouldn't do any good,' said Boris gloomily. 'It's nothing to do with her or her father. In fact that's why they're after me: to discredit her father if they can. I say "they" but really it all boils down to one man: Andropov, the boss of the KGB.'

'Surely Brezhnev can deal with him?'

'Yes, he can, but the reign of Brezhnev is coming to an end and the vultures are gathering. Andropov is the man most likely to succeed him. And he's right into his election campaign . . .'

Boris gave a short mirthless laugh at the thought of an election. 'The man who knows the most dirt about Brezhnev will be the next winner. Andropov is already hard at work spreading the idea among the old guard that he is a pure Communist and just the person needed to clean up all the corruption. He is piling up dossiers on anyone who has the remotest connection with Brezhnev, accusing them of diverting state money for their personal gain. I've got a dossier all to myself. Mine's marked "Boris the Gypsy, Galina's lover". I wonder what they've put on yours?'

It was a chilling thought. As he said it I wished once more that I was out of it all and safe at home in London. I forced a laugh and said, 'Come on, you're making all this up!'

'You think so?' said Boris with contempt.

'But how can you know?'

'I know,' he snapped, 'because I fuck Galina Brezhnev. That's how I know. When I'm lying there afterwards, flaked out with a prick that feels as if it will never stand again, my ears still work and so does my memory. I encourage her to talk because if she goes to sleep straight afterwards it won't be long before she wakes up and wants it again.

'She's a mine of information, is our Gala, especially during one of her drinking bouts. I remember it all because the things she tells me may well save my life one day. They're not just little things she dishes out: I reckon I know more about the intimate thoughts and diplomatic tricks of Comrade Brezhnev than anyone in the whole of Moscow. And when I say Moscow, that means the whole of the Soviet Union.'

I tried to change the subject, afraid that I might learn things that would stop me too being allowed out of Russia. Boris spoke as though he could read my mind. 'Don't worry, Stanley, you've really got nothing to fear.

I know I shouldn't be telling you these things, but I give you my word I will never reveal to anyone that I told you anything. Try and be like my priest – hear my confession, Father Stanley.' He put his hands together in a gesture of prayer. 'Oh, Father, I am afraid, and I want you to know, in case I suddenly disappear.'

'Bless you, my son,' I said. It was a weak attempt at humour and it did nothing to stop Boris's confession.

'Let me tell you a secret – but first give me your word you'll tell no one.' I agreed. Boris was silent for a moment as some more people came close and he did his trick of pointing out the sights again until they had gone. When he spoke it was barely audible: 'A little while ago, Gala made me try out some pill she'd heard would give me an erection twice the normal size. I don't know what it was, but though it didn't make my prick any bigger, it produced another effect that Gala absolutely adored – the damn thing wouldn't go down. Gala went completely crazy, bounding about on me for what seemed like hours. It hurt like hell, I can tell you. I think I'd still be there now if she hadn't finally decided that even she had had enough!

'Well anyway, we were lying there afterwards and she suddenly said, "Boris, why don't you and I get away from here together. I've got lots of cash and jewellery – we could lead a dream life somewhere else." It was quite clear she was talking about the West. The idea appealed to me of course, but you never know with Gala – perhaps she was just trying me out. So I told her that she shouldn't talk that way. I had the feeling she was testing me, but maybe I was wrong.

'The other night she came up with the same idea again. I don't know – could she get us both out? Could she up and leave Russia just like that? She hinted that I'd need to give her lots and lots of diamonds. Gala would do anything for diamonds. But did she mean it? I can get diamonds if that's all she wants. But will that get me out? Or is it just another of her wicked games?'

I awoke late the next morning. I had slept badly and had dreamed about a great scorpion surrounded by fire, trying to escape and, when it couldn't, taking its own life by stinging itself tail to head. I didn't need an analyst to explain the dream, though it would have been more apt perhaps if I had dreamed of a snake because I could feel myself being enmeshed in the coils of a drama that was certainly not the thing for me. In Russia the Ministry of Culture and Gosconcert officials had praised my efforts. I was treated well by all and sundry. Even the embassy in London had helped me. Now I was putting everything at risk just because of a gypsy called Boris. It was stupid and ridiculous and, above all, dangerous. I would back out . . . return home and never visit Russia again. That made sense. But my resolution lasted only until I remembered that today was the day I was to lunch with Galina Brezhnev. There was no backing out of that.

I already knew a great deal about her, not just from Boris, but from Irena, who had gleefully filled me in on her background when I had asked. Even when young, she said, Galina had been nothing but trouble. She had studied literature at the Pedagogical Institute in Dnepropetrovsk and had shocked her teachers there with her promiscuity. Then she had gone on to the Kishinov University to study philology and if she hadn't been Brezhnev's daughter she would never have been allowed to finish the course. Things got so bad at one stage that Brezhnev himself, who was then the Party chief in Moldavia, asked some students to try to get his daughter to join the Komsomol, the Party's youth organization. But Brezhnev's daughter had refused to join the Party!

By then Galina's mind was fixed on other things. The Shapito travelling circus had visited Kishinov and she had seen something she wanted. She went to every performance just to watch the strong man Yevgeni Milayev, whose speciality was lifting a dozen people at once into the air. They say his genitals matched his strength. Galina got her first real instruction in sex from him and when the circus left town Galina went with it. Soon afterwards she married Milayev and Leonid and Victoria Brezhnev didn't see their daughter for a year. When she returned she brought a daughter with her and left the little girl for her mother to look after. The marriage to the strong man lasted eight years. They had evidently fought most of the time and Galina was livid that her parents always took her husband's side. Irena said they had good reason: Galina's private life was already a not-so-private scandal. But Galina stayed with the circus after the marriage break-up and had every kind of lover, from trapeze artist to lion tamer.

Brezhnev became Chairman of the Praesidium in 1960 but even then Galina didn't stop being an embarrassment to him. In fact, when he took her with his wife on a state visit to Yugoslavia, her behaviour and wardrobe caused so much of a stir in the press that he never took Galina abroad with him again.

However, she continued to visit foreign countries with various circus troupes and no one there knew that she was the daughter of one of the most powerful men in the world. Whether her father realized she was travelling abroad no one knows, but she had the protection of the Director of Administration for all circuses in the Soviet Union, Anatoli Kolevatov, and in the circus world he was all-powerful. In return for this cover, Galina is said to have saved the Kolevatov family from more than one nasty scrape.

Then Galina fell in love again. Despite the fact that she was by this time thirty-five, she chose a 'toy boy', the twenty-year-old Igor Kio, whose real name was Renard. His father was an Emil Renard, who put on a famous illusion act using the stage name Kio. When Emil senior died, his two sons, Emil and Igor, carried on the act. It was while they too were on tour that Galina met Igor. One day they turned up together in the Crimea, at a little local register office and demanded the formal registration of their marriage. The poor director of the register office could hardly argue with Brezhnev's daughter, so he declared them man and wife and issued the necessary documents.

Apparently Brezhnev was furious when he heard, and this time he did do something about it. A military transport aircraft landed close to the place where the couple had set up home and some large men in civilian clothes got out and descended on the Kio household. Galina was flown back to Moscow, where some more strong men were waiting in a black Volga to take her home to Papa. Poor Igor was taken to the local police station where he was issued with new documents which made no reference to the marriage, and was told to forget the whole thing.

Irena said that Galina had been more or less her father's prisoner after that. He had tried in the past to tame her with kindness. Now he did it the hard way. Galina had to live with her parents, be home by a certain time each night and was eventually sent back to university to get herself a degree in literature. She didn't like it but she had no choice and she consoled herself with affairs in the afternoons when she was meant to be attending lectures.

She soon found herself a regular lover. The fact that he already had a wife and children didn't worry either of them. He was Yuri Churbanov, a lieutenant-colonel in the KGB, dealing mainly with simple policing. He was seven years younger than Galina, but very ambitious – above all things he wanted to be Brezhnev's son-in-law – and very soon he and Galina were married. Brezhnev didn't object to her third husband – after all, anything was better than those dreadful circus people, and this man at least was a police officer. Yuri's career prospects became excellent as a result of his marriage and he soared up to be Deputy Minister of the Interior. But within the same short time Galina was already having affairs and everyone in Moscow knew that Brezhnev's daughter was an easy lay.

In some ways I looked forward to meeting her. By all accounts the woman was a nymphomaniac and I was curious to know what she would look like. Boris had said I would be surprised, but would not be drawn further. I thought of Russian courtesans, Catherine the Great, and I wondered . . .

My phone suddenly rang. 'Hello, Mr Laudan,' said a voice I instantly recognized as that of a deputy director of Gosconcert. He said he had called to see if I needed anything – were the contracts in order? I knew immediately that his call was no innocent enquiry; he too was checking up on me. I told him what he wanted to hear, that I was off to a lunch engagement where a VIP would be present. It never does any harm to tell them what they already know.

'Oh, how nice,' said the voice at the other end. Was there a note of sarcasm there? 'Well, have a good time and don't miss the plane, will you? And have a good trip. We look forward to seeing you again soon.'

'Thank you, Igor Igorovich,' I said, and put the phone down.

His attitude of studied politeness worried me. I knew he was a KGB plant in Gosconcert and one of Andropov's top men. Andropov had his men in every department of state and as Gosconcert was part of the Ministry of Culture it merited special attention. People like Igor Igorovich, who had no experience of any cultural medium, were put in as 'deputy directors'. But even Igor Igorovich had someone keeping an eye on him, something I found out quite by accident. Not all KGB personnel were placed in top jobs. They were often among the 'little people' in big organizations. Though I didn't know it at first, Alla, who had acted as interpreter for us on one of the earlier tours, was one of them. She was on the payroll of Gosconcert as a secretary and interpreter, but she seemed to move freely into all sorts of departments and was always terribly busy. I found out what she really did when she asked me a question about something that I had raised only in a confidential business letter to the General Director of Gosconcert, Supagin. He couldn't have read that letter or commented on it to anyone as he was on holiday in Sochi when I wrote it and had not returned by that time.

The phone rang again. This time it was Boris, but he wasn't downstairs. 'I'm sorry,' he said, 'I can't pick you up. But I have laid on a taxi. Make a note of the number: 4782. It's a white Volga. It will be waiting for you outside the Metropole in a few minutes. Sorry about this but some of my guests have arrived early. They don't stick to the rules here you know – especially when the food and the booze are free . . .'

'Don't worry,' I said. 'We have people at home like that too!'

The taxi turned off Marx Prospect, then into Gorki Street. After a while it turned into Uskaya and stopped in front of the block where Boris lived. I tried to pay the driver, but he said he had already been paid. I pressed a tip on him anyway, then entered the block. I was surprised that there seemed to be nobody on duty downstairs. I took the lift to the fifth floor, and as the lift doors opened, there was Boris. 'Don't get involved in any unnecessary conversations.' He hissed the words out of the side of his mouth in the approved American gangster tradition.

His guests were in the dining room and looked as though they had already downed a few. Boris announced me very formally and took me round to each one in turn . . . 'The director of the Mkhat Theatre, the famous Moscow drama . . . you know . . . the director of the Puppet Theatre . . . and this gentleman is the brother-in-law of Comrade Chairman Brezhnev . . . and now I have the pleasure to introduce you to the nine-times Hero of the Soviet Union, Admiral of the

Fleet, Anatoly Fedorovich . . .' I mumbled something about how honoured I was to meet them.

Boris showed me to my chair. It was second from the end of the table. The chair next to mine was empty. I looked around and could see at once that Boris hadn't held back on anything. The table flowers were magnificent and the starters for the meal were already on the table: plate after plate filled with cold meats, fish, salads, freshly-baked rolls, bowls of caviar, exotic cheeses. It was a remarkable sight: as much a display of wealth as food. The bottles of vodka were in solid-silver coolers and some of the flower bowls had the dull gleam of gold.

When the door to the dining room opened everyone at the table got up and virtually stood to attention. Galina Brezhnev had arrived.

SEVEN

Galina Brezhnev was quite unlike what I had imagined. First of all, she was in her forties. Somehow I had expected a nymphomaniac to be younger. She was about five foot six, slim, but with a full bosom under a white embroidered silk blouse which she later told me, with some pride, had come from Paris.

She had an air about her. She entered like a ruler granting an audience to a few of her subjects. With arrogance and great style she came to each of us in turn and offered her hand to be kissed.

She was bedecked with jewellery. On the front of her blouse was a huge diamond brooch, there were diamonds on her hands and in her ears, and fighting for attention amid all the sparkle was a gold chain looped several times round her neck with an antique gold watch on the end. By Russian standards her clothes were luxurious.

Her dark chestnut hair was combed back from her face. Her eyes were light brown under very heavy eyebrows, obviously inherited from her father, and her skin was good. She wore very little make-up and a few freckles peeped through. Her nose was straight and firm like her chin. She had full lips over a good set of small teeth which showed when she turned to Boris, saying, 'So this is our friend, the impresario from London!' I kissed her hand in the traditional continental manner, lifting it high.

'I have heard a lot about you,' she said and sat down beside me. 'Only good things of course. Get me a gin and tonic, will you?' As I busied myself pouring her drink, she said in a deliberately loud voice, 'One can recognize a gentleman at once by the way he attends to a lady – not like these uncivilized peasants all around us!'

The guests who had just been insulted reacted as though she had been joking, but she didn't let up. 'Look,' she said to me, 'you see what we are lacking in this country. No one has any manners. In Russia education is done with muscles, not brains . . .'

This was obviously too much for the Mkhat director. 'But Galina . . .'

'Don't you "Galina" me! You can't talk. I saw the last play you produced. It was dull, appalling. It had no finesse at all. You think that's good – it was crap!'

The director sat there speechless, like a small boy who had been dressed down by the headmistress. The admiral decided it was time to impose his authority. 'How can you say such things! We have such beautiful music, ballet too . . . the whole world admires us for it!'

'The whole world!' sneered Galina. 'The whole world gets on with things. I'm talking about civilization, not just a couple of ballets and a few composers. Oh, it makes me sick! Here it is always the same. We never make any progress . . . but we have the admiration of the whole world . . . for what? For our music and our ballet! Is that all?'

'Indeed not, Madame.' I blundered into the fray. 'Russia has just made a very great stride forward – I have it on very good authority that Boris Buryatsa has just joined the Bolshoi. The whole world will now admire your opera too!'

It worked. Everyone laughed, including Galina who embraced me ostentatiously and kissed me on both cheeks. I detected the strong fragrance of Chanel No. 5. She opened her beautiful crocodile handbag and took out a ten-kopek piece, solemnly handing it to me. 'A joke like that must be paid for,' she said. 'It is an old Russian tradition!' She was on her third gin and tonic and the atmosphere had eased enough for Boris to say to Galina, 'Now don't you start seducing him! He's a married man.'

It was time for lunch. As the waiters served the food I realized why there were no staff on duty in the foyer: they were all up here waiting on Boris and his important guests. And noting down everything that was said, no doubt. That thought made me even more aware of the power that Galina Brezhnev had. Only she would dare to voice such critical thoughts in public.

When coffee was served, Galina took my hand and led me over to a settee in a corner. I looked at her long fingers with nails beautifully polished and manicured, and found myself admiring her shapely stockinged legs. I understood what so many men saw in her.

'How tall is your wife?'

'A little taller than you, Madame.'

'Don't call me Madame,' she said, pouting like a little girl. 'Call me Gala, that's what my family calls me. Is your wife like me?'

'Just a little taller.'

I had had too many similar conversations in Russia not to know what Galina was after. She wanted dresses from the West. I knew I was right as soon as she opened the crocodile bag again. She took out an antique gold watch, very similar to the one just above her cleavage, and pressed it into my hands.

'Please give this to your wife with my best regards. I do hope I shall meet her one day.'

I kissed Galina's hand as a gesture of thanks.

'Get me another gin,' said Galina, 'and then come back here. We have lots to talk about.'

I cut back on the gin this time and could see from her expression – a slight narrowing of those brown eyes – that she thought it was too weak, but she said nothing.

Instead she asked how my business in Moscow had gone. 'Did you arrange everything for Khatchaturian's tour?' I told her about my meeting with the composer and the difficulty I was having in getting permission from Gosconcert to make a recording for television of his concert in London. 'There's so much red tape,' I sighed. She nodded, apparently in agreement.

When Boris offered me a lift back to the Metropole, everyone made a move except Galina. Boris told her that he wouldn't be long, and it was clear that when he got back he would find her in his bed.

Even so, Boris didn't seem in an hurry. He pulled in to the pavement close to the hotel, switched off, and started questioning me: 'What were you talking about all that time? What did she give you?' I showed him the watch and suggested that perhaps it would be best if he took it and gave it back to her.

'Don't be bloody mad! Give it back to her! She'd go crazy! You can't return one of Galina's gifts, not if you value your life, you can't!'

Boris probed further about my impression of Galina. I was not at all sure what to say. 'I think she's probably very fond of you in her own way . . .' I let my voice trail away.

'Very fond of me! I'm bloody sure she is . . . like a black widow spider. She's spun a web right round me! She's even planted Zvigun on me. That's her uncle – the one I introduced you to. What a bloody old bore he is! He's there to keep an eye on me when she has to be elsewhere. I have to play cards with him all the time and I have to let him win too. I don't care about the money – what's a few roubles here and there – but if only he wasn't such a bore. God, I'm sick of the whole thing. I have to get out! If I don't, I'll go mad.' Boris lapsed into silence. Then suddenly, 'Well, I suppose I'd better get back. She'll be lying on my bed now, working herself up for Boris Big Prick.'

We talked about my imminent departure and I was

amazed to see tears in the man's eyes. I hoped Boris's homosexual tendencies were not beginning to focus on me. He rummaged in his handbag and pulled out a stone the size of a small egg. It was light mauve in colour and beautifully cut. 'Here,' he said, 'this is for you as a going-away present. It's an alexandrite. I bought it from an old lady in Leningrad a few years ago. I paid 10,000 roubles for it . . .'

I told him I couldn't accept it.

'All right,' said Boris, 'then you can have it for the same price. It's more than five carats.'

'Look, Boris, I haven't got any money and I don't know anything about alexandrites!'

He pushed it into my pocket even so and I gave up. I got out of the car and went off with a cheery, 'See you in August!' Boris hesitated and then shot straight out into the Moscow traffic. A trail of horn blasts finally faded away into the distance.

My plane was scheduled to leave Moscow a little after 5 p.m. and I was to be taken to the airport by a deputy director of Gosconcert. Dima Ratov picked me up at 3 p.m. and asked questions all the way to Sheremetyevo. He was planning to visit London in the near future to attend some auditions and was very excited about the whole thing. He pumped me remorselessly about what he would find and what he could do on his first trip to England. I was glad when we pulled up at the airport entrance and Dima started taking my luggage out of the boot of the car.

As I was trying to disentangle the rest of my possessions from the back seat, I felt a discreet touch on my shoulder. A very large man, who looked exactly like a plain-clothes policeman, stood before me. I felt a chill of fear which disappeared as soon as I realized that no policeman, off duty or not, would make an arrest with a large bunch of carnations in his hand. 'These are from Galina Brezhnev for your wife. With hearty greetings.' Dima's mouth dropped open as the big man (it was

Galina's chauffeur) walked off to his car.

Gone were Dima's hundred and one questions and in their place was a sort of silent respect. He insisted on carrying my bag all the way through the terminal to customs and even beyond before finally saying goodbye. As I settled in my seat in the aircraft, I felt completely drained.

When the plane took off, the bouquet of flowers fell from the seat beside me to the gangway floor. I picked them up quickly and noticed some writing on the white band which held the blooms together. It read: 'Dear Maestro. It was a great pleasure to meet you. Permission has been granted for televising the concert. Best wishes. Gala.' When I fell asleep a short time later, there may well have been a smile on my face. That permission meant a great deal to me. Now I could not lose money on the Khatchaturian venture.

London didn't offer much respite from the machinations of Moscow. I had only just got back when the phone rang. It was the Cultural Attaché of the Soviet Embassy in London. What on earth could be so urgent that he had to ring me almost as soon as my feet touched British soil?

He wanted to arrange a lunch for the next day at the Green Park Hotel. I agreed at once just to get him off the phone. But though I asked him what it was about, he hedged and said how much he was looking forward to hearing all about my trip to Moscow.

I arrived a little early at the restaurant in the hotel and toyed with a drink while I waited for Tamar Starayev. I wondered for the thousandth time that morning what this lunch was all about. I knew him quite well, but that in itself wasn't reason enough to meet so quickly after my return. His predecessor had evidently left a good report on me in the files, because it wasn't long after his arrival in London that Tamar was offering me help with cultural exchanges between our countries. In turn I helped him find comfortable accommodation in London and he seemed grateful ever afterwards. He and his wife were extremely hospitable and made pleasant hosts at many dinners in their London home. But I couldn't help feeling that it wasn't just cultural matters which interested him. He often tried – unsuccessfully – to steer me into political arguments, but I wanted to do business with the Russians, nothing else. That is why I determined once again that I would have nothing to do with Boris on my next trip to Moscow.

Tamar arrived and greeted me Russian-style with kisses on both cheeks. His opening gambit was to insist that the lunch was on him and after making token protests I let it be. He had scarcely settled on his seat before he asked, 'How was your trip to Moscow?' I took the question at face value and gave him a résumé of the Khatchaturian visit, including the arrangement to televise the concert. It was obvious I was only telling him things he already knew, and I was more deeply aware of Galina Brezhnev's powers there in a London restaurant than perhaps I had been in Boris's flat in Moscow. When I had finished there was a pause and Tamar said, 'It all sounds very good for you. I am happy to hear it.' After that there was another pause which stretched into a long silence.

Finally he said, 'Look, I asked you here to lunch to prime you about one or two things. You have to go and see the ambassaor. You are to have coffee with him at ten o'clock tomorrow morning.'

I disliked the tone and said that I might not be able to make it. 'I'm pretty certain I have another appointment for tomorrow morning.'

Tamar got the message and realized he had gone too far. 'I'm sorry,' he said. 'I didn't mean it like that . . . this is very difficult for me . . We're friends . . . but I do have to ask you some questions about Moscow.'

I started to protest, but he held up a warning finger. 'Don't make it difficult, Stanley. I know you have friends in Moscow and that your private life is your own, but you must tell me about it.'

'What is there to tell? I was invited by some people – performers, musicians, composers – to a party or two. We enjoy each other's company, it breaks up the deadly monotony of Moscow . . . you know all about that, don't you . . . we have a drink, a joke, perhaps a song . . . and that's all there is to it!'

It wasn't the answer he wanted. He tried again. 'You know, Stanley, we trust you . . . After all, we know a lot about you . . . and we'd be unhappy if our friendship was marred by some petty gossip, perhaps even false accusations . . . I know what the ambassador is going to ask you so I wanted to see you first . . . then I can add more detail if necessary to anything you tell him. Did anything else happen in Moscow?'

I forced a smile. 'Oh, I see . . . Well, I think I've told you everything except that I met Galina Brezhnev.'

'Now you're talking. Tell me more.'

'There's nothing to tell. I met her casually at a lunch with a friend of mine and apart from some standard conversation about the weather and so on, we didn't talk much at all. I found her very pleasant.'

'And?'

'And nothing. That was it. I didn't sleep with her if that's what you mean.'

The crudity of my remark cut the conversation and the question dead. Tamar's smile disappeared. I don't know if he had intended to broach the matter of Boris, but he did not push it any further. It would probably not be too good for his career if he was known to have been inquiring too deeply into Galina's sex life. The lunch did not last long after that. Tamar confined himself to conventional small talk and he left with a formal handshake.

The invitation to meet the Soviet Ambassador was

duly confirmed and Mr Lunkov received me promptly at ten the next morning. Lunkov was a devoted Communist and an extremely good diplomat. He was a master at pushing the Party line – *détente* and peace were the current front-runners – and he was popular on the diplomatic circuit. I had found him very tactful in our previous meetings and he had never tried to discuss anything with me except my work and show-business in general.

This meeting began just as usual. He poured me coffee and asked about the Khatchaturian contract. I told him about all my talks in Moscow. He listened, asked one or two questions, and when I had finished, said, 'That all sounds fine. But enough of business. How did you find Moscow?'

'As always,' I replied, 'I enjoy Moscow enormously. I think it must be the cold fresh air – in some way it seems to recharge my batteries!' He laughed and seemed relieved that I had given him the opening he wanted.

'I expect that's true,' he said, 'but then you know our country better than most. That makes you a lucky man! That sort of experience is very valuable to you in your job.'

I nodded agreement, and wondered exactly where this good-life lecture was leading. Something was hanging in the air; something he hadn't yet articulated. He started up again: 'You know, Mr Laudan, you have our complete trust. You are, as you have said in the past, trying to build a bridge over troubled waters . . .' He smiled at the aptness of his phrase. 'You are introducing your artistes to us and arranging for our artistes to perform in Britain. This is important work and, rest assured, we appreciate it. But I must tell you quite openly that as you travel such a lot around our country you must be careful about the people with whom you associate.'

There – it was out. Though he hadn't actually mentioned Boris by name, there was no doubt in either of our minds whom he meant.

'This is, of course, not an official complaint, it's just a reminder . . . a mild caution, you understand.'

I understood all right. But I didn't fall into the trap of rushing to explain or excuse myself. I merely said, 'You may rest assured, Your Excellency, that I am fully aware of what you mean, but I can also assure you that when I am in Russia I am minding my own business and nothing else.' The meeting was clearly at an end. I left the embassy firmly resolved that this really was the finish of any connection with Boris, even if it meant losing an important contact like Galina Brezhnev.

I discovered later that at much the same time as I was being warned by the ambassador, Boris and Galina had lain in bed, exhausted after strenuous lovemaking. Galina had suddenly started to tell Boris what she had learned from her father that very lunchtime.

Leonid Brezhnev had apparently just finished a private meeting with Gromyko and Chernenko when the latter had asked to speak to him 'about a family matter'. He had started by asking if Brezhnev knew what was being said about Galina? To Boris's horror, Galina had mimicked Chernenko: 'I am talking about her affair with a gypsy called Boris Buryatsa!' Gala had laughed when she felt Boris shiver.

He had felt even worse when Gala reported that her father had replied, 'Oh that, I know all about that from Gala herself. You know that Gala's always had these affairs since her early teens: ballet dancers, sportsmen, entertainers, I've lost count. They don't last long. It doesn't matter.'

When Chernenko had persisted, saying it was bad for the country to have people talking about her and it was even worse to have her name linked with this gypsy – 'he's a playboy, a flashy nobody, a cheat and a thief, an empty clown, an insult to decent workers' (Boris remembered each description with great clarity) – Brezhnev had replied, 'What do you want me to do about it? If I kill the bastard, or have him arrested, it will only turn the thing into a major scandal . . .'

Chernenko had then suggested that Brezhnev should talk to Galina about it and tell her to go to the south until things quietened down. And that is exactly what Leonid Brezhnev had done. He had talked to Gala about it over lunch, and suggested that she dump Boris and go into hiding for a while in the south where she might meet someone more suitable.

Boris was shattered by these revelations. It sounded like the beginning of the end. If Gala dumped him, the KGB would be on his doorstep in no time. But when he had asked Gala what she wanted him to do, she had laughed and said that for a start the 'flashy nobody, the empty clown' could behave like a 'decent worker' and satisfy the woman in his bed. But this time Gala had gone too far and despite all her efforts, nothing she could do would rouse Boris again that afternoon.

EIGHT

The evening before I was due to return to Russia my wife and I were invited to the Soviet Embassy for a cocktail party. It was nothing really special, just another party. It was graced with some top politicians, but most of those tucking into the free food and drink were union leaders and officials from boroughs sympathetic to the Marxist ideology, and others expecting high positions 'come the Revolution'. Most of them spoke in ignorance of Russia, and even the Soviet Ambassador had a glazed look as he was buttonholed by one union leader who insisted on calling him 'brother', and 'comrade' by turns. When the drink really took hold it became 'brother comrade'.

The ambassador eventually made his excuses and came over to join us. After the usual pleasantries he told me, apparently apropos of nothing in particular, that Tamar Starayev was being replaced and was returning to Moscow. He was sure that Tamar's replacement would work with me with the same enthusiasm.

I don't know why I found this piece of information sinister, but I wondered why the ambassador should have made such a point of telling me about Tamar. Was it just because we had worked together? Was he warning me again about the company I kept in Russia? Was Tamar to keep an eye on me in Moscow? I slept badly that night and woke full of gloomy thoughts about the tour.

This gloom resisted even the cheery meetings with Robert Young and the band at the airport. We arrived in Moscow and were to have the usual overnight stop in the city before setting off on tour. As soon as I got to my room I rang Boris and asked him to come to the hotel as a matter of urgency.

I don't know what he expected but he seemed to be there almost as soon as I had put the phone down. I asked him to sit down and from my wallet I took the alexandrite he had given me. I pushed it across the table towards him and said: 'My dear, dear friend . . . I'm sorry but I am going to have to return this stone to you. I don't want to cheat you by paying you only ten thousand roubles for it when its real value is many times that. I couldn't do that to a friend any more than you could.'

Boris looked completely confused. He had known all along that the stone was not genuine. I had found out by taking it to the Geological Museum in London where an expert had told me that its only value lay in how skilfully it had been faked. Boris decided to bluff it out . . .

'No, no, my friend, I have committed myself and I never go back on my word. Ten thousand roubles I said and ten thousand roubles it will be. As I told you, I bought that stone from a very old lady. God knows how old it is . . . she said it came from her great-grandmother . . .'

'You're a lying bastard!' The suddenness of my fury checked Boris. 'Don't you ever try to play such a trick on me again, you lousy cheat!'

Boris hung his head.

Before he left I gave him two dresses for Galina which my wife had bought from one of the most expensive couture showrooms in London. This somehow added to the unreality of the whole situation. Here was I handing over dresses from London to a cheating gypsy so that he could give them to his mistress, the daughter of one of the two most powerful men on earth!

When Boris left I watched him walk to his car which was parked defiantly right outside the hotel. He would come to a bad end, of that I felt very sure. He was born to cheat, to lie, to steal, his good looks merely camouflaging his true nature. Despite everything, I felt sorry for him and hoped that he would make good his escape.

Kiev, delightful in summer, was our first stop on tour. The chestnut trees were in full bloom and the long lines of them, running right through the town, were beautiful. Everything there seemed to go well. The theatre was modern, almost luxurious, and our audiences seemed to enjoy themselves enormously.

Our interpreter for the tour was a Jewish girl called Rosa. The Russians tend not to allow the same interpreters or guide to work with a group of foreigners for very long in case personal relationships develop. At first I was as reserved with Rosa as she was with me. But gradually relations thawed and we became friends. She had a good sense of humour and laughed easily at the jokes we made. One of the standards was to say when entering a new hotel room for the first time, 'Testing, testing, one, two, three, are you receiving me?' I sometimes wondered what those listening in made of Rosa's open laughter at this sort of thing. I hoped for her sake they thought she was stringing us along.

Our next stop after Kiev was Riga and on our free days we were driven to the Baltic coast. The white sandy beaches with pine forests extending behind were very pleasant, particularly as we were in the middle of a heat wave. The beach we liked best had soft sand and was not much used. Robert Young would sit down and stretch out to sunbathe, but within a very short time a group of women would have gathered round him.

One of the women was different from all the rest. She was beautiful and slim and, unlike her plumper, better-endowed sisters, she brought her boyfriend to the group around Robert. Her swimming costumes – which she changed frequently – were all very Western in style and her other clothes would not have been out of place in the South of France. She was called Tiyu and she called her boyfriend Sasha. Rosa saw me watching her. 'Not bad,' she said, 'not bad at all! She looks all right, but watch that Sasha. Don't get too familiar with him – he looks like a black marketeer to me.'

One evening there was a knock at my hotel-room door. It was Tiyu and Sasha. 'We came to invite you for dinner.'

'I'm sorry,' I replied. 'I can't, but thank you for asking me.'

Sasha almost put his foot in the door and said, 'Please don't say no. We know a very good restaurant. You'd like it, you really would. We'd like to have you as our guest.'

Robert was busy that evening so I decided after all to accept. The restaurant was in the very smart Hotel Latvia. The music was unusually soft, the food excellent, and the atmosphere very European, complete with cabaret. It was when coffee was served that Sasha made his move. He pulled his chair close to mine and spoke in little more than a whisper.

'I have been wanting to meet you for a long time.' It was an odd way to start as he had only met me by chance on the beach. His next words were even stranger and made me sit up in alarm. 'I'd like to give you a nice present to take home with you: it's a very old icon.'

I told him that I didn't want it and that it was expressly forbidden to smuggle icons out of Russia.

He saw he had gone too far too quickly. 'OK, OK, but

I would like to give you something to remember us by...'

'What on earth for?'

Sasha launched into a long story about how he and Tiyu were to be married in December and couldn't find anywhere to live, how Tiyu was six months pregnant, and how the housing authorities would not give them a flat. 'They have just built a brand-new block in the centre of town. We'd be so happy to live there...' His voice trailed away and he looked pleadingly at me. I didn't see what that had to do with me and said so. 'You could arrange it,' said Sasha.

'Don't be silly,' I replied, thinking the man must have mistaken me for someone else. 'I'm in charge of a British show on a tour of the Soviet Union – I have nothing to do with housing.'

'But you know someone who could.'

I got there before him, but the idea was still extraordinary.

'Who's that?' I asked.

'Boris Buryatsa... Gypsy Boris.'

'You're joking! You mean to say that Boris, back in Moscow, can fix you up with a flat here in Riga?'

'He could do it anywhere, in any town you like to name.' Sasha was quite matter-of-fact about it. 'Of course, he doesn't do it all by himself. He has help.'

I found the idea of Boris and Galina running a sort of estate agency – Buryatsa and Brezhnev Limited – faintly absurd. I seemed to be in an Alice-in-Wonderland world. The only thing to do was humour him. 'If you are so sure that Boris can fix it, why don't you approach him directly – yourself?'

'I did,' he said flatly, 'but he wants too much. One hundred thousand roubles.'

A lot to ask, even for Boris. One hundred thousand was about thirty years' salary for someone like the Director of Gosconcert. I sat in silence for quite a while. I suddenly felt very, very tired.

'What makes you think I can help you?'

'They say he listens to you. You can persuade him to take less. We can scrape together 30,000 roubles at most.' Tiyu's eyes were fixed on me and a solitary tear ran down her cheek. It was enough to make me say, 'I'll try. Next time I see him.' She leaned across and kissed me.

When I got back to the hotel, Rosa was waiting outside my room. She looked angry, and appeared to know exactly where I had been, and with whom. 'What the hell have you been up to?'

I offered her a drink, but she brushed me aside and marched into the room. I poured myself a large vodka and told her what she wanted to know. I defended my agreement to speak to Boris by saying that perhaps Tiyu was entitled to the flat because she had been born in Riga.

'Don't talk rubbish, Stanley. You know perfectly well why you agreed. She turned her big brown eyes on you – and you fell for it. You'd better watch out – you're going in over your head!'

Rosa looked round the room. I expected her to say 'Testing, testing . . .' but instead she whispered, 'It's time you and I had a little talk . . .' I followed her out of the room and down the stairs like a naughty boy. Rosa strode into the middle of the deserted square and then swung round to face me.

'Now,' she said, 'I'm going to tell you this once and once only and I'll deny I ever said anything like it if you dare mention it to anyone. Stanley, I like you, and the way things are going, you are going to get hurt!'

I had the impression that this was a speech she had rehearsed many times before in her mind.

'Can't you see that Boris Buryatsa and Galina Brezhnev are into all the rackets – and have been for a long time. She'll do anything to keep him. Anything the gypsy asks, she does – even if she has to get it out of Papa with the full works – tears, the lot. You brought her a couple of dresses from London . . .' How could she have known that? '. . . but that is chickenfeed. They have accumulated a fortune not only in roubles but in foreign currency – dollars, pounds, pesetas – you name it, they've got it.' Rosa was in full flood, passionate, and deeply angry.

'I don't give a damn about the money – though others mind very much. What I care about is the fact that they are cheating poor Jews out of everything they own, pretending that they can help them to emigrate to the West. It's all lies: they have never helped anyone get out, and they never will. And you, you allow yourself to get involved with them!'

She was crying now and as she thumped her breast with her clenched fists she looked like an avenging angel.

'I have no doubt you've had warnings from others in the past, but perhaps they were less direct. I'm telling you straight, don't get involved any more with your gypsy friend. Oh yes, he can be charming and sometimes generous to those he thinks can be of use, but whatever he gives – however small – he only gives to get big returns.'

I tried to protest that I was not getting involved in any of Boris's schemes, but Rosa would have none of it.

'Not involved? Can you honestly say that you haven't taken any presents from him? Well?'

I repeated – without conviction – that I was just an observer, not a player in Boris's games.

'Stay like that,' said Rosa, 'and some of your real friends in Moscow might continue to trust you.'

'What's that supposed to mean?'

'You don't need any explanations, Stanley . . . Anyway, that's enough, I'm tired. I'm going to bed.' And with that she turned and led the way back to the hotel. Things were never the same again between us.

I had a late breakfast in my room the next morning. It had taken me a long time to get to sleep, and time and time again my mind had fixed on the same question: who exactly was Rosa? KGB? Something to do with Jewish resistance? Just an interpreter who had overheard too much? Why did she feel free to issue warnings to me?

This speculation was interrupted by a soft knock at the door. It was Sasha. 'Come in,' I said, resignedly. 'Have some coffee.' Sasha was nervous. He kept shifting position in his chair while I poured the coffee and then stood up and checked if the main door was closed.

'I wouldn't tell this to anybody . . .' he began. I had an insane desire to laugh, being well aware that he might be talking to the whole KGB. 'I have to get that flat. I'm desperate. I'm going to tell you something about Boris. When he realizes you know, he will be sure to help me with the flat. I'm only doing this for Tiyu, you understand . . .'

'Of course.' What a creep, I thought.

'Do you know a young man called Sima?'

'No.'

'Never mind,' said Sasha, 'it's only a matter of time before you do. He's always around Boris, calls himself his brother, but he isn't really. He's gay, like Boris. Galina found him. She likes to watch them at it before she has Boris herself.'

Sasha swallowed his coffee in one gulp and pushed his cup forward for a refill before going on.

'I met this Sima in Moscow quite by accident. I was having a meal in the restaurant and he was at the next table. I expect he thought I was another gay because I was alone. He introduced himself and we found we had some mutual friends – business contacts really. After a while he asked me if I wanted to earn money, big money. He said he would introduce me to his brother, Boris Buryatsa, who would cut me in on a money-making scheme which he was sure would interest me.'

So far, I thought, this had the ring of truth about it. The homosexual making a pick-up in a restaurant and discovering that, though his new friend wasn't of the same sexual persuasion, they did at least share the same criminal contacts.

'I met Boris Buryatsa the next day at his flat – I was in Moscow for only a few days on business. He said that the next day we would go together to Klin, a little place about forty kilometres from Moscow. You probably know it, it's quite a tourist attraction because of the Tchaikovsky Museum there – in fact there's nothing else, really. Boris said he'd pay me 50,000 roubles to make the trip and, as you can guess, I was hooked. The plan was to rob the museum at Klin of the original score of *Swan Lake*. He said they'd been working on the plan for over a year. He'd got someone inside to disconnect the alarm system and all we had to do was to lift the glass case and walk out with the manuscript. The manuscript was to be replaced with a replica forged down to the tiniest detail from a photograph. It would take years for the theft to be discovered.

'Boris said the original was worth millions of dollars and he had someone waiting in Moscow to take the manuscript out to Switzerland and from there it would go to a collector in America. Part of the money was to be paid in Moscow, the rest to go into a Swiss bank. He made it all sound so easy and well-planned.

'We left for Klin at ten the next morning. The museum opened at eleven. Boris had told us to stay close to him and form a screen when we reached the *Swan Lake* case. He made the switch so well that I hardly saw it and I was right beside him. The next ten minutes seemed to take hours. We moved around pretending to be interested in the other exhibits until Boris signalled us back to the car. He's a cool customer – he seemed to have no nerves at all.

'We drove back to Moscow and Boris let me out at Gorki Street. He said he would contact me very soon to give me my share . . .'

'And did you get it?' I asked, guessing the answer.

'No, I didn't. Oh, Boris thought he was clever. And he was, up to a point. But he wasn't bloody clever enough. When the manuscript was examined it was found to be a worthless copy – obviously the real score had been locked away in a vault somewhere.'

Nothing Sasha had related encouraged me to stick my neck out for him. I failed to see how my knowing about the attempted robbery at Klin would make any difference to Boris. 'I'm sorry, Sasha, I can't help you.'

'But surely you can see what sort of a shit Boris is. I risked my skin for him – and never got a rouble for it. Now when I want a favour, he asks me for 100,000 roubles!'

'That's nothing to do with me.'

'But you promised, you promised Tiyu!'

'I didn't promise anything. I merely said I would try to have a word with Boris about your problem. But the whole thing stinks and I'm not getting involved in any of it!'

Sasha started pleading with me. He offered money. He even offered Tiyu. Then there was another knock at the door, harder and firmer than the one which had heralded Sasha's arrival. Rosa was obviously surprised to see Sasha but managed even so to greet him politely. She turned to me and asked, 'Did you sleep well, Boss?' The form of address was clearly adopted in an attempt to get our relationship back on to friendly terms.

I tried to play the game. 'Not really, Rosa. I dreamed of you, and my wife gave me a black eye!'

'Just my luck,' said Rosa, looking questioningly at Sasha behind his back.

'Can you give Sasha a couple of tickets for the concert? He came all this way to ask me for them. He's just found out all the tickets went long ago.'

'Such confidence,' said Rosa, in a very Jewish tone, but she gave him two anyway and ushered him to the door at the same time. Sasha looked back at me just before the door closed and the pleading look was still there. I turned away.

'What the hell did he want?'

'Tickets.'

Rosa had something of the look of the previous evening in her eyes. I revised my answer. 'Well, he really came about the flat again. He wants me to intervene with Gypsy Boris.'

'Boris, Boris – is there no other name! Let me tell you something about your new friend Sasha. He is nothing more nor less than a cheap criminal. He's nearly as bad as your beloved Boris.'

'Beloved Boris be damned! He means nothing to me!'

— NINE

Looking back, it seems that I learned more about modern Russia in those two days than in all my previous visits. I now found myself looking everywhere for signs of corruption. In the past I had accepted all the small-scale corruption – the bribes to waiters and concierges – as a matter of course, but now I had discovered that what went on at the bottom of the heap was bigger at the top.

The next stop on our tour was Leningrad, the most civilized city in Russia. Architecturally, the city is beautiful and the old part has not changed since it was built by Peter the Great nearly 300 years ago. Time stands still in this part of Leningrad, and a stroll through the park and streets on a quiet afternoon is like a journey into the past.

The quality of the city is matched by its people. They are surrounded by culture and it seems to rub off on them. We were treated royally in Leningrad and the response from our audiences surpassed all our expectations. We were showered with gifts – champagne and flowers – and when we left the city hundreds of fans crushed against the windows of our train and girls cried hysterically.

After Leningrad our return to Moscow was rather depressing. My gloom was partly alleviated by the fact that Gosconcert had booked us back into the Metropole, which I interpreted as a reward for a job well done. Certainly the tour so far had been a huge success and our last two weeks were to be spent in Moscow.

I wasn't to be left in peace for long. On the morning after our arrival there was a phonecall from Igor Igorovich of Gosconcert. Instead of asking me to come and see him at his office, he invited himself to lunch. 'I will be there at one o'clock.' He didn't bother to ask me if it was convenient. When he had first done this to me many months ago, I had been irritated and upset, but now I was used to it.

Igor Igorovich was prompt as usual. This time he brought with him a present for my wife. It was a bottle of rare pepper-vodka and he took a long time explaining to me how difficult it was to get and how special it was. Conversation then ranged from ice-hockey – his favourite sport – to the stars I planned to bring on future tours. It wasn't until after lunch that he embarked on what he had really come to say.

'How was the tour?' The familiar question always seemed to herald some sort of reprimand. I braced myself. 'Did you meet any interesting people?' The second step in the ritual dance. If he had known about Sasha and Tiyu beforehand, his face gave nothing away. 'What about here in Moscow?' – the interrogation procedure less disguised now – 'I understand you've met a singer from the Bolshoi?'

'Oh, you mean Boris,' I tried to sound casual, 'yes, I've met him a few times. He's quite a character. Very hospitable. He introduced me to Galina Brezhnev . . .'

Igor's poker face gave way to consternation and in my mind I immediately demoted him several ranks in the KGB.

'Did you talk to Galina Brezhnev yourself?'

'Of course. We were at lunch together. She is very charming, isn't she?' Igor's expression revealed that they did not move in the same circles.

'Indeed . . . she is . . .' he faltered.

Lunch – and the interrogation – were at an end. I had survived better than I had expected. After he had gone, I wondered if I should tell Boris of all the approaches which had now been made to me. The net was apparently closing around him, or at least Andropov's men were becoming bolder. I had very little time to consider the matter: Boris suddenly turned up at my hotel room with a package in his hand. He motioned me into the corridor, evidently feeling it was a safer place to talk.

'It's for you,' he said, handing me the package. 'From Gala – a going-away present.'

I pulled at the wrapping and found myself holding a very beautiful old icon.

'Gala says you are to hang it on the wall in your home so it will always remind you of Russia.'

'Boris, I can't possibly accept this! First of all it's too valuable and you know what the customs do to people who try to smuggle icons out of Russia!'

Boris held up his hand like a traffic policeman. 'No problem. Here.' He handed me a piece of paper covered with stamps and signatures. 'It's all legal and above board. This is an authorization from the Ministry of Arts giving you permission to take this icon out of Russia.'

I thought of the *Swan Lake* manuscript and wondered if I was looking at a forgery. 'I don't want it, Boris.'

'Look, it's nothing but a return gift. Gala was so delighted with the dresses you brought her that she's decided to give you a little something. Anyway, I told you before – a gift from Gala should never be rejected.'

I started to walk back to my room, thinking absurdly that Boris looked too well-dressed in his grey suit and silk shirt to be standing in a hotel corridor.

'Don't go yet, my friend. I want to tell you about my new plan to get away from all this. I have to tell you about it before you leave for London. Maybe you can help me . . .'

'No, Boris,' I almost wailed, 'I don't care what it is,

this time I'm not helping anyone.'

'But you hardly have to do anything.' Boris spoke as though he were hushing a fractious child. 'Just introduce me to a few girls.'

'Girls?'

'Foreign girls.'

'Foreign girls! What the hell are you up to?'

'I want to marry a foreigner.'

'You've got to be joking. Galina would kill you!'

'She won't find out till it's too late.'

He outlined his plan calmly and matter-of-factly. If he could find a girl from the West and marry her he would be able to return with her as her lawful husband. Even Galina would be unable to stop him. The right of a married couple to be together was an international law to which even Russia had to conform. I questioned the Soviet Union's regard for international law and suggested that the KGB would find a way to keep him if they wanted to. But Boris had convinced himself that the plan would work.

'You can easily help me, Stanley. If you bring over some female artistes on your next tour, I can marry one of them.'

'You don't think you'd have to fall in love with her first, or anything like that?'

Boris grinned. 'Don't worry, my friend, I know how to charm a girl . . . See you in November!'

When I returned to Moscow in early November I was surprised to find a welcoming committee waiting. Irena and Rosa were there and also Alla, whom I had asked should never be attached to our group again. I made a mental note to have a firm word with Igor Igorovich about her at the first opportunity.

The band were packed into a mini-bus and I climbed into a waiting Volga with the three women. Irena of course lost no time in filling me in on all the gossip. She also warned me that I would not get much sleep that night since Boris had arranged a welcoming party at the Veteo Club for us. Rosa didn't flicker at this news but I was unhappy with the idea, mainly because it had become traditional for me to organize a party for the performers on the evening of our arrival and I resented having arrangements taken over by Boris. It was also irritating the way he loomed each time I set foot on Russian soil.

When Rosa had settled everyone into their rooms she appeared at my open door and asked: 'Are you very tired?'

'Why?'

'Oh, nothing – it can wait . . .'

I could see that it couldn't. 'Come on, what's happened?'

'A lot,' she said, 'and the sooner I get it off my chest the better.'

We moved out on to the balcony, safer than my room, and the story unfolded. 'There's been a terrible row between Galina Brezhnev and the gypsy . . .'

It turned out there had been a series of thefts at the Bolshoi, mainly from the dressing rooms. At first the members of the company had been reluctant to bring in the authorities to investigate, but gradually more and more things had begun to disappear. Then the principal tenor had missed a gold lighter, a treasured present from La Scala opera company, and had reported the theft to the Bolshoi director. Eventually suspicion had fallen on Boris, mainly because his so-called brother Sima had taken to turning up during rehearsals, which was when most of the things had disappeared.

Galina had come to hear about it and had been furious with Boris. She had accused him directly, knowing that the thefts coincided with his joining the Bolshoi. When he had denied it and tried to put the blame on Sima, she had had him banished from Moscow.

I asked Rosa what he was doing back in the city and giving us a party that very evening.

'No one really knows exactly what happened. All we know is that the missing items mysteriously turned up again in the dressing rooms and Boris was allowed back. He and Galina seem to be together again, but things aren't quite the same as before. For one thing the KGB aren't so wary of him: he's pushed it too far and they think he'll do it again. And next time maybe Galina won't want to save him.'

'What are they saying in Gosconcert about all this?'

'I don't know,' Rosa confessed, 'they wouldn't talk about it, but when I told Igor Igorovich about the party, he said he would be there.'

There was a long silence as I tried to absorb the implications of everything Rosa had told me. Eventually she said: 'I thought it important that you knew all this before you see Boris tonight.' I nodded in agreement, not really knowing why I agreed.

The party at the Veteo was to take place in the back room of the club. Boris stood at the door greeting everyone effusively. His clothes were all early Hollywood: white tuxedo and frilly silk shirt. Inside the club a great horseshoe of tables sagged under the weight of food and bottles. I saw Igor Igorovich immediately. He looked quite relaxed, but not relaxed enough to suggest he was off-duty. I suspected him of being a secret womanizer; his eyes followed the women round the room and more than once a lascivious smile crept over his face.

As the party wore on I was surprised to see him engage Boris in conversation. Igor was apparently confident enough to be seen talking to Galina Brezhnev's lover in public. It didn't seem quite right somehow: the hunter chatting with his prey. Perhaps relations had changed, just as Rosa had suggested.

The evening was a great success. Boris had arranged a cabaret of gypsy singers and the atmosphere became pleasantly sentimental. As I left I thanked Boris for the party. 'I hope it's just the first of many,' he said, walking with me to the street. 'It's one way of meeting foreigners, and I'm still determined to find a wife who'll get me out of this hell-hole.'

We walked on, but Boris was clearly ill at ease. 'I've had a lot of problems lately – Galina's been behaving like a pig.' There was no need for me to say anything – he was going to tell me in any case.

'I trust people too much. I'm too kind-hearted, that's my trouble. People take advantage of me. That idiot brother of mine dropped me right in it.' Boris then lapsed into such a long silence that I wondered if he had thought better of confiding, but he was presumably deciding on the most appropriate version of events.

'Sima got up to his old tricks – this time at the Bolshoi. I won't go into it but it nearly finished me off with Gala. She thought it was me, and all the time it was that bastard Sima! I've sent him away from Moscow. Perhaps a stay on the outside will teach him how good he had it with me! I can't tell you what a nightmare it all was. First of all Gala didn't believe me – can you imagine – she wouldn't believe me! And when she finally did she had to use all her influence to clear my name and convince that idle swine, her uncle Zvigun, that I had nothing to do with it! In the end he had the bloody cheek to ask me for a huge loan and only when he got it did he tell Gala that he had known all along it wasn't me! Anyway, all the things that were stolen were given back. A lot of bloody fuss about nothing!'

Since I was not meant to know about any thefts, I was about to question Boris, but he suddenly pointed to a window in the Intourist Hotel where a naked woman was standing by the curtain. 'Look at that! They're all on the job in there – bunch of KGB tarts. I wonder what happens to all their hookers when they're past it?' And he strolled along as if trying to work out some kind of harmless puzzle.

'Did you invite Igor Igorovich to the party?' he said after a while.

'Of course not,' I said. 'It wasn't my party.'

'Then he invited himself.'

'Does it matter all that much?'

'Like hell it matters! He's not just there to enjoy the free drinks, you know!'

'Well, I don't mind him. He doesn't bother me. I'm always on quite good terms with him, which is just as well since he's the one who signs my contracts.'

'You only know him as an official of Gosconcert,' said Boris, angry now. 'I know him for what he is: a colonel in the KGB. He knows damn all about the arts – his job is to keep tabs on everything that happens in and around and underneath Gosconcert. You don't get to be a colonel in the KGB by being a nice guy at a party. And you say you don't mind him! You'd better be more careful, my friend, the man's dangerous.'

The comic aspect of being warned by both sides at the same time was not lost on me, but I stuck to the same line with Boris as I had with Igor Igorovich.

'Look, Boris, I don't care if he is a colonel or a field marshal, he's an official of Gosconcert and that's that. I am not concerned with anything other than showbusiness.'

Boris smiled indulgently as though I were an innocent child. 'Oh, how refreshing it is to listen to someone like you. Pity we can't all be as romantic – dare I say complacent? – as you seem to be. Perhaps you'll have a change of heart when I tell you how many questions Igor Igorovich asked me about you! He was very interested in you!'

It was a trick, surely it was a trick. But my face betrayed alarm and Boris saw he had scored.

'Ah, you're not so confident as you make out, are you, Stanley? Perhaps you have something to hide?

Perhaps you're a British spy . . .'

I mumbled in protest but we had reached the front of my hotel. Boris turned round to face me: 'You know how it is, don't you? Tonight he asked me a lot of questions about you, tomorrow he will ask you about me. And that's how it goes on here. Round and round – until someone gets giddy and says the wrong thing!' He then embraced me in his usual friendly way and said, 'See you in Vilnyus. I'm not letting you out of my sight, Stanley. I'll be popping in on your tour and – who knows – you may soon be bringing me my wife!'

The next day started badly. The phone woke me and I grabbed the receiver angrily to hear, 'Car number 684 is waiting for you outside.' At first I thought someone was phoning the wrong room, but then I recognized Boris's voice.

'Forget it,' I said. 'I'm still in bed. You woke me.'

'Sorry. Breakfast in forty-five minutes, OK?'

'No, it isn't bloody OK.'

'It'd better be,' said Boris and hung up.

Car number 684 was waiting outside. It was a fairly modern Volga by Russian taxi standards and the driver was more polite than usual. As soon as I was inside he said, 'Gospodin Buryatsa asked me to tell you, sir, that I am to take you, not to his apartment, but somewhere else, so don't worry about the route.' As a result, I naturally took a keen interest in where we were going. We went across the bridge and took a turn towards Lavrushinsky Pereulok, where the car stopped. Boris was waiting in front of a building. He muttered some apology about the sudden invitation and looked nervously up and down the street. I looked too, thinking that perhaps I had been followed, but the street was completely empty. As we entered the building Boris said, 'You're going to see someone you know at breakfast.'

'Who?'

He said nothing in reply and we walked up the stairs to the first floor. He took a key from his pocket and opened the first door on our left. I hesitated and he took my arm, saying, 'It's just a friend's flat I occasionally use for convenience.'

There was a smell of fresh coffee. And of French perfume, Boris opened the inner door to a large room and sitting behind a table directly in front of me was Galina Brezhnev. She studied my face for a moment or two and began to laugh. 'It's not a ghost, Mr Laudan, it's really me!' I kissed her hand and she motioned me into the seat beside her. Boris sat down opposite.

As he did so a door at the far end of the room opened and a maid came in carrying a tray with eggs and bacon and fresh rolls and butter. The atmosphere was strained and we started our breakfast in silence. Galina was the first to speak, not in her normal imperious way, but in a coquettish, little-girl voice: 'It was my idea to give you this surprise, Maestro . . . you're not angry with me, are you?'

'Not at all, Madame. I'm happy to see you at any time.'

'Any time,' she repeated, smiling sensually, 'that sounds interesting. But perhaps we had better stick to daytime. After all, both of us have our nights reserved – you for your beautiful wife and I . . . well, you know how dangerously jealous gypsies can be!' She looked coyly at Boris, whose face was completely devoid of dangerous gypsy jealousy.

'I understand you are going on tour tonight?'

'Yes, Madame.'

'Oh, do stop calling me Madame. I've told you before you must call me Gala. All my friends do.' She leaned towards me and the scent of Chanel No. 5 was overwhelming. She came closer, deliberately offering a clear view of her ample cleavage. I wondered what was next.

'Boris seemed reluctant to approach you so I decided

to ask you myself, face to face. Will you do me a personal favour?'

'I'll try.' (What else could I have said, I asked myself, already trying to justify my answer.)

'I believe you have some concerts scheduled for Volgograd?'

'Yes...'

'Well, it's like this ... at this time of the year, Moscow is very short of certain things ... diamonds for example. There are plenty of jewellery shops but no diamonds. Volgograd is different. As you know, it is the "City of Heroes", and because of that it is better supplied with all sorts of things, better goods than we see even in Moscow...'

My mind pushed a panic button. Surely she couldn't be asking me to buy her diamonds? My face gave me away.

'Don't look so worried, Maestro.' I made an effort to comply but my anxiety grew as she continued.

'Volgograd has no diamond shortage. Diamonds are plentiful there and, by happy coincidence, you are going to Volgograd.' Boris shifted uneasily in his chair. 'Our interest,' she said, nodding to Boris, 'is in buying diamonds. And we want you to buy them for us.'

TEN

The scene had obviously been carefully rehearsed, Galina now used her most authoritative tone.

'Why are you looking so worried? It's no crime to buy jewellery. You can go into a jeweller's and buy anything you wish, provided you have the money, of course. The reason I am asking you is that I trust you and you happen to be going to Volgograd where diamonds are plentiful. What could be simpler? If Boris or any of his friends were to go they would have to get a travel permit and everyone would become suspicious and . . . well, it would just be a lot of bother . . .'

They both sat and looked at me. When I said nothing, Boris took up the story: 'Look, Stanley, it is all terribly simple. The manager of the main jewellery store in Volgograd is our friend. She has been keeping aside for us all the diamonds bigger than one carat. There's nothing illegal about that. Do you understand?'

I didn't trust myself to say anything, so I just nodded. It was at this moment that Galina produced a leather attaché case from under the table. Pushing the breakfast dishes aside, she laid it before me. 'Here you are then, here is the money. All you have to do is to give it to Maya Borisovna, the manageress . . . with my compliments, of course.'

I finally found my voice: 'I'm not sure about this at all. I'm a guest in your country. I don't think I should run the risk . . . even for you.'

'But there's no risk.' Galina sounded quite overbearing now. 'I don't know what you are worrying about, I really don't. You are not being asked to do anything against the law. Would I ask you if it were a question of that? It is purely and simply because you are going to Volgograd with your artistes and you will make a perfect courier. Remember I shall always be grateful for your kindness . . .'

At that she flipped open the lid of the attaché case and the packed ranks of notes lifted up a little at the release of pressure. 'Half a million roubles,' she said, and stroked them lovingly before adding, 'Take good care of them.'

They both stood up and Boris embarked on vows of undying gratitude which I quickly interrupted: 'I don't want your gratitude, Boris, but I do want an assurance that this won't rebound badly on my work here.'

Galina replied for him: 'I give you my personal pledge that in future you will have no obstacles to your work in Russia. And if you're still worried when you get to Volgograd, take someone with you – take that interpreter girl of yours, Rosa what's-her-name, if you like. There's no reason for secrecy . . . after all, it's common practice in this country to find things in other cities if you can't get them in your own.'

'But the money? How can I explain the money?'

Galina sounded exasperated: 'You don't need to explain the money. Who's going to ask you about the money? Just take the case and hand it over as I've told you. Take the package she gives you and Boris will pick it up from you later.'

'In Vilnyus,' said Boris.

I could see no way out. I wanted no part in their schemes, but one word from Galina and all my work could be stopped. In fact, one word from her and I might never get out of Russia. When I finally agreed to do what they asked, Galina embraced me. Her perfume almost choked me, and now her voice was warm as she whispered in my ear, 'You won't regret it. I promise.'

We left Moscow late that night and started rehearsals for our show, which was to run in Leningrad for a few days. I kept the attaché case by my side at all times. After Leningrad we went on to Volgograd – better known by its former title of Stalingrad. Its name was changed back in 1961 after the truth about Stalin started to emerge. I wondered how long it would be before all the places named after Brezhnev would suffer the same fate.

The Volgograd concerts went well and to my immense relief the other business also went smoothly, as Galina had said it would. I was now the possessor of a sizeable package of diamonds. Shortly after I had collected the stones, an official price rise for all jewellery was announced and I suspected that I had been instrumental in a diamond speculation.

I now felt hopelessly enmeshed in Boris's and Galina's schemes and so it was with a mixture of relief and regret that I found Boris already booked into the hotel in Vilnyus when we arrived. He was full of himself, claiming to be in Vilnyus 'on very important business', but I suspected he was there simply to pick up Galina's parcel. 'You do have something for me, don't you?' he asked within moments of our meeting, and I was very relieved to hand the package over. He didn't open it, just weighed it in his hand.

I told him that I was never going to do anything like that for him again and that I wanted to have no more contact with him. Boris was placatory. 'All right, all right,' he soothed, 'we won't ask you again. Don't worry about it. But surely we can still be friends – you are my only real friend in the whole of Russia . . .' He was a charmer, but his real concern in maintaining contact seemed to lie in his desire for a suitable marriage partner. 'You won't mind if I flirt with your

English ladies, will you? I assure you, sir,' he posed, 'that my intentions are honourable – I intend to marry the girl!' I laughed and Boris knew that he had won.

It was then that he delivered the *coup de grâce*. 'By the way,' he said casually, 'I have a message for you from Gala. She said to tell you that in view of the fact that your work in the cultural field is so much appreciated, the government has instructed Gosconcert to arrange more frequent tours for you and to arrange better financial terms and general conditions to be specified in your contracts.' He paused in anticipation of my grateful response.

'You bastard!' I exploded. Boris looked stunned, quite unable to understand that the last thing I wanted was to have Galina Brezhnev as a benefactor and to worry constantly, as he did, that her beneficence was dependent on the precarious health of her father. In the past I had always tried to keep as far away as possible from politics and corruption. This had been successfully achieved, until I met Boris, which had marked the start of a pattern of scheming and deceit. The realization that everything I had worked for now hung in the balance made me furious.

'You can tell that slut that when I want her help I'll ask for it! I don't want to be involved in any more dirty business. I came over here to organize a tour, not to act as postman for your shabby deals . . .'

'Maestro, don't take it like that. Gala was only trying to help. You know how things operate here – it's only natural to want the luxuries of life. Surely you understand that the only way we can get such things is to take a piece for ourselves of whatever is going.'

'I understand no such thing. I know all about the average Russian's struggle for the better things in life, but you're talking about criminals. And they're not peculiar to Russia. They're the same in every country in the world. And no matter where they are, I don't want any part of them.'

After that I had nothing more to do with Boris during his stay in Vilnyus. I had discovered that his brother Sima was also booked into the hotel and I assumed the two of them were up to no good. I acknowledged Boris if I met him in the hotel, but apart from that I avoided him whenever possible, and he in turn seemed to keep away from me.

Despite this, I couldn't help knowing what he was up to in Vilnyus. Every now and then I would spot him at parties in the company of flower dealers from the south – mainly Armenians and Georgians – who had flown to the cold north to sell their flowers at enormous profit. The dealers were easy to spot, not only by their swarthy skins and dark complexions, but from the way they spent their money in restaurants so freely. Often I would catch a glimpse of Boris surrounded by a group of dealers and holding a small velvet cloth which I knew contained diamonds. The stones were of a size and quality that those visitors could never find in their own regions no matter how much money they had. Sima was never part of these secretive sales and I wondered where Boris sent him to keep him out of the way.

I assumed that the diamonds he was selling were those I had collected for him, although that didn't seem to make sense. Or had Galina lied to me? That was more than likely – but I had certainly believed that the diamonds were to be brought back to her in Moscow. Was Boris double-crossing her? Or had this been the plan all along? Which brought me, as it always did, to the biggest question of all: why did Galina Brezhnev entangle herself in these shady dealings? That didn't make sense either . . . However dependent she was on Boris's sexual favours, this seemed too high a price to pay for such services. Surely she could have all the jewellery she wanted, so why go to these lengths to get more?

Why did Galina need so much money, anyway? She

was rich. She wanted for nothing. And yet she obviously felt the need for more. The question came at me again and again. The only logical answer was one that I almost hesitated to consider. Was Galina Brezhnev planning to defect to the West? Was she planning to follow in the footsteps of Svetlana Stalin, but with the difference that all that money in a Swiss bank would mean a life of luxury for her in the West?

Or could she be planning to escape with Boris? If that were the case then all the stories Boris had told me were just camouflage to throw the KGB off the scent. They must know that he was trying to get out. But supposing that was not the exact plan? Supposing Boris was leading the hounds one way and all the time he and Galina were going to slip out by another route? Once in the West they could live in great style on the money they had smuggled out – and the stories they could sell to the press would earn them another fortune. I could almost see the headlines . . . RED GALA AND HER GYPSY LOVER ESCAPE TO WEST . . . RED PRINCESS AND GYPSY PLAYBOY FLEE KGB. Everything a tabloid could desire.

Speculations such as these were uppermost in my mind when I stood one afternoon in Market Square in Vilnyus watching the frenetic bargaining in the busy market. Suddenly I became aware of Boris standing a few yards away. As I turned, he gave me a friendly wave and came over to stand beside me. He kept looking at his watch and seemed to be waiting for someone or something. After a few minutes a car pulled up right beside us and I backed away as a group of gypsies poured out of the car and advanced on us. The tension eased only when they all started embracing Boris and kissing him on the cheeks. It was quite unnecessary for Boris to explain to me 'these are my gypsy brothers'. Without saying any more he drew one of them away and left me with the others. I could see that Boris was up to his old tricks again as he took some papers from his attaché case and handed them to the gypsy along with a large bundle of roubles. They rejoined the group, there were more embraces and kisses, and then they all climbed back into the car and were gone.

I walked away without a word but Boris tagged along. When we came to the newly built opera house he said, 'Hang on a moment – I want to buy a ticket. They're doing *Yevgeny Onegin*. I'd like to see what the Lithuanian production does to it.' When he came out of the booking office, he said, 'I know you don't want to hear about my problems, but I feel I owe you an explanation . . .'

I cut in quickly: 'I don't want to hear. You don't have to explain anything to me. I'm not interested!'

'But you must hear what I have to say. It's important. And if "they" should ask you, you can tell them.'

It sounded sinister and so I listened. 'The young man I spoke to was my cousin. My real cousin. I gave him papers to keep in a safe place. They are my insurance policy. If things go wrong here, they may save my life.'

'Why tell me this?'

'Because you may be useful one day. If the KGB ask you one day – and they can be awfully persuasive – you can confirm that the documents exist . . . because you saw them just now, didn't you? Even if you don't know exactly what is in them!'

I began to understand. Boris didn't do anything for nothing. Now he had made me part of his insurance policy. 'The gypsy could let you down.' I spoke in a flat voice. I was sick of Boris.

'Yes he could, but that's not the only copy. I'm not a fool. Another one is already being smuggled out to Turkey, and there's another . . . but it's best that you don't know about that . . . Suddenly he came to a halt. 'Well, I'd better say goodbye, I'm catching the Moscow train tonight.' He bent over to embrace me and went off in the opposite direction with a final 'Don't forget you're going to find me a wife!'

I didn't answer and instead stood wondering why he

had bought a ticket for an opera he wouldn't be there to see. As I watched him go I felt almost sorry for him. I suddenly had the irrational feeling that he could be walking to his death. I looked after him until he was just a small shape at the end of the long street and I couldn't help noticing a man get up from a bench long after Boris had passed. The man was joined by another and they went down the street together. Boris was being followed. At a distance, but definitely followed.

ELEVEN

Once back in London, I had plenty of time to think things over. I told my wife everything that had happened and we wondered whether it was wise for me to go back at all. But I was not at that stage of life where I could retire even if I wanted to; I was financially dependent on the tours continuing.

Viewing things from a distance only strengthened my belief that Boris's days were numbered. That in itself made him more dangerous to everyone around him. He was like an animal who had the cage door open, but who could see the keeper coming to close it. And his stupid flaunting of wealth – the shirts embroidered with diamonds, the flashy foreign cars – coupled with his refusal to live within the law, acted against his own interests, not only infuriating the ruling class, but turning ordinary Russians against him.

Galina could offer him only limited protection. The 'friendship' she had arranged for Boris with her uncle Semyon Zvigun afforded him few safeguards, even though Zvigun was First Deputy of the KGB. It was common knowledge that Zvigun and Andropov, the KGB chairman, were locked in a power struggle and Andropov seemed to be winning hands down. In such a battle Boris was small fry and I had no doubt that if it suited Zvigun, Boris would go to the wall.

When I flew into Moscow soon after Christmas there was an invitation to a 'Zasidalka' or New Year's Eve party waiting for me at the Metropole. It was to be held at the House of Artists and although the invitation had come to me via Boris, I knew that the party would be attended by many showbusiness people and that it would be sensible for me to go.

First of all, however, I had to meet with officials from Gosconcert and arrange new tours. The meeting with Supagin, the General Director, was short. He gave me his usual boring lecture about how wonderful Russia was, thanked me for the good work I had done on behalf of the USSR State Concert Agency and then let me go. There was no attempt to question me. Any grilling would be left to those officials who were in Gosconcert for that purpose. Igor Igorovich was the main Gosconcert inquisitor at the time and so it was with a mixture of apprehension and resignation that I found myself ushered from Supagin's office into the plush rooms of Igor Igorovich.

He greeted me like a long-lost friend with a bear hug and kisses on both cheeks. 'My dear friend,' he said, 'what would you like to drink?' I asked for coffee and knew that he would offer something stronger. I refused and held out for coffee. From his opening remarks I knew that I was due for an interrogation. He started by saying that I was 'a true friend of Russia' and did not need to be reminded like other foreigners of all the important things. He then proceeded to remind me of them.

It was clear that I was now talking to Colonel Igor Igorovich of the KGB, a fact which my irritation made me show him I was aware of. 'Colonel . . .' I started, but got no further.

'No, no, no,' he faltered, momentarily thrown off balance by my mention of his rank, 'don't call me that. Call me Igor Igorovich.' He quickly got a grip on himself and returned to the questioning: 'I've said it before, my dear Stanley, and I'll say it again: you are a clever man . . . and your last tour went exceptionally well.'

The softening-up tactics were ill-disguised. 'Did you enjoy Volgograd?' He couldn't have cared less whether I enjoyed it or not and I waited to hear what he really wanted to know. 'And how was Vilnyus?' Some inflection of his voice told me that this was it. News certainly travelled fast.

I decided to short-cut the colonel: 'I met Boris in Vilnyus.'

'Oh yes?' said Igor Igorovich, his voice just a shade too casual, 'What was he doing there?'

'I don't know,' I said. 'He was staying at the same hotel, but apart from casual meetings I didn't see very much of him at all.'

'Didn't he come to your concerts?'

'I didn't see him there. He didn't come backstage, if that's what you mean.'

Igor toyed with a pencil. 'Was he alone?'

'I believe he had his brother with him. Sima something or other . . .'

'What was he doing?'

'I don't know. And I don't know what all these questions are about . . . Colonel.'

The reference to rank did not have the same effect as before but he was clearly nettled. 'Questions? Just gossip, that's all. Gossip between friends . . .'

'Well, it may be just gossip to you, Igor Igorovich, but it seems like close questioning to me. I'd be much happier if you would limit our "gossip" to matters concerning my business here. My business is entertainment – showbusiness, that's all. I won't get involved in your domestic affairs. I'm a guest here and that's all. It's up to you to keep your house in order, not to use me to do so.'

Igor Igorovich sat silent for a few moments before saying, 'That's fair enough,' as though some training manual had told him not to enter into arguments with foreigners, 'but I'm sure you understand that we have to be alert and careful with outsiders. Not all of them love Russia and the Russian people the way you do . . . I will tell you what is on my mind, but before I do I want to assure you that you are held in very high esteem.' He then embarked on a fulsome five minutes on the importance of doing business with Great Britain, the great home of art and culture, and my own place in furthering exchanges. 'We think of you as one of us: after all you did go through a large part of the war with us, and I feel I can be more open with you than with some others who visit us. I want to talk to you frankly, if you will allow me, about your acquaintance with Boris Buryatsa. I also want to tell you a few things which may influence your association with him . . .'

He had finally arrived at the whole point of the meeting. He now looked every bit the KGB colonel. His eyes were cold and gone were the protestations of everlasting friendship voiced only moments before. 'You see, there are a lot of stories going around about this man, but they are not exactly my business. You are my business and when Boris Buryatsa does things which affect you, then that becomes my business. Up to now, as far as I know, you have done nothing wrong. But I have reason to believe that your association with Comrade Buryatsa might – I stress might – lead you astray, and it is my duty to give you fair warning.'

'Warning? Warning about what?' I heard myself sounding so guilty that I shut up at once.

In reply, Igor Igorovich opened the drawer of his desk and took out a single sheet of paper. 'This is a letter I received a few days ago. You will see that it is unsigned, but the person who wrote it is no uneducated peasant. Since it concerns you, you may read it.'

I felt sure that Igor Igorovich must have noticed my trembling hands as I held the letter, but that hardly seemed to matter when I read the contents. It denounced me and alleged that I was involved with

Boris in huge currency fiddles. It went on to say that I was also working with one Igor Igorovich and was smuggling large sums of money out of the country for him. The next paragraph said that Boris had organized a ring of currency dealers who swapped roubles for foreign currency, paying visiting businessmen from abroad high black-market rates in exchange for dollars and sterling. I was named as one of the men from abroad who deposited their profits in overseas bank accounts.

I finished the letter and started to read it again. The accusations were grave: the black-market rouble exchange is considered a most serious crime. All sorts of thoughts raced through my mind. Who had written the letter? It must be someone who knew me. Did the idea of currency smuggling come from someone who knew about Galina's attaché case full of roubles? I didn't know what to say to Igor Igorovich, who was studying my face carefully. In the end I played for time: 'Well, what do you make of it?'

'I'll tell you. The paragraph about me is not a worry: I know how to handle that. What does worry me is you. I'd like to believe that you have nothing to do with this, but there is an old Russian saying, "When you chop onions, you smell of them" . . . I hope now you can see why my questions were so pressing. I don't think I have to say anything more, do I?'

'No,' I said. 'I only hope you believe that I have nothing to do with any currency swindles – I suppose you must believe it, otherwise you would have acted very differently. But I repeat that I am here only to take part in cultural exchanges.'

Igor Igorovich smiled a mirthless smile. It was clear that the interrogation was over.

I walked very slowly back to the hotel. The letter had shaken me. Who could have written it? Who would want to write it? And then another thought – had anyone really sent it to the KGB? Or had the KGB written it themselves? A trick to see what I would do? That was the most worrying of all, because it would mean that Igor Igorovich really did believe I was involved. I cursed Boris and I cursed Galina. I was sure my trip to Volgograd as their courier had something to do with the letter, plant or no plant.

To my horror, Boris was waiting for me in the hotel foyer. 'Have you lunched yet? No? Come on then.' He seemed in very high spirits. He wore a well-tailored sheepskin coat which had certainly been made outside Russia, and on his head a sable cap. There were new flashy rings on his fingers. He looked like something out of a musical comedy. I made the ritual protests but his big hand fell on my shoulder and he propelled me out of the front door. 'Come on, I've cooked a special gypsy meal for us. It's fantastic – the sort of thing we serve at gypsy weddings. You'll love it!'

As he hustled me across the pavement to his car, I looked frantically up and down the road to see if anyone was watching. And they were: wherever Boris went people stared at him and today was no different. 'What's the matter with you, Stanley?' he asked, as he pulled straight out into the traffic. Brakes squealed and horns protested behind us. 'Why are you so nervous?'

For a moment I thought of saying, 'No reason in particular. I've just been interrogated by a colonel in the KGB and people are accusing me of currency swindles with you . . . and here I am ten minutes later going off to lunch with you.' But I didn't say any of it. The madness of the situation depressed me and there seemed nothing I could bring myself to do to stop it.

When we went into his apartment I saw through the open door to the dining room that the table was laid for four. The smell of cooking was heavy on the air. 'You're in for a treat today,' said Boris. 'I've given my housekeeper the day off. I wanted to show you how well I can cook!'

He led the way into a room which opened off the hall on the opposite side to the dining room. 'This is my study,' he said. The walls were entirely wood-panelled and under the window was an antique desk, too delicate for anything but the lightest of letter writing. In front of the desk there was a seventeenth-century chair with a seat of shiny silk, and on the walls a selection of old prints, mostly showing Napoleon's retreat from Moscow. An apt choice for Boris, I thought.

Boris anticipated my reaction to the splendour. 'I suppose you're wondering why I should want to leave all this and escape into the unknown? But these treasures are dead and cold, and I want to get to things that are alive and free. Any one of these things can be replaced – or you can buy something similar. But who is going to sell me freedom?'

His language was so dramatic and extravagant that I felt a great urge to laugh. But Boris obviously didn't find it a subject for laughter; there were tears in his eyes.

The drama wasn't over. Boris ostentatiously locked the door behind us, and then hesitated. He really should have been on the stage. He said, 'I'm going to show you something that only Gala and I know about!'

'Don't, Boris,' I said immediately, and the alarm in my voice was genuine. 'I don't want to share any secrets. I told you I don't want to get involved. Don't show me anything.'

Boris took no notice. 'Look,' he said, and shooting his cuff like a conjuror, pressed one finger on a carving on the side of the desk. As he did so, part of the wooden panelling behind it folded back like a Venetian blind to reveal red bricks in the wall. He then pressed on the bricks, which moved out and sideways, revealing the front of a modern steel safe.

'Very impressive,' I said. 'When did you have that done?'

'Some time ago,' said Boris, clearly pleased with himself.

'Who did it for you?'

Boris's look of pleasure faded just a little at my question. 'An engineer from Finland . . . pity about him. He was a chronic alcoholic like the rest of them. He fell from an express train and was killed . . .'

This remark in itself aroused no suspicion. Tales of drunken Finns were legion in the Soviet Union. People said they only came to Russia to get drunk – because the rate of exchange was so favourable. But Boris continued: 'The police weren't altogether satisfied about the cause of death and marked it down as "foul play". One of them even told me that they thought it was a contract killing by a special hit-man.'

'Why on earth would anyone want to kill a Finnish engineer?'

'Don't ask me!' said Boris, and closed the subject. I had the impression that he suddenly realized he had said too much. I didn't push him.

'Why show me these things, Boris? Surely it isn't sensible to let anyone know?'

'I'm not worried,' Boris grinned. 'Anyway, you are already regarded as an accomplice of mine, guilty by association. But don't worry, you're not a Soviet citizen, so they can't punish you for my sins!'

As he spoke he fiddled with the lock and when he stepped back the door swung wide and revealed an Aladdin's cave.

The shelves of the safe were stacked with foreign currency, bundle after bundle of used notes, mostly dollars on one side and a mixture of marks and pound notes on the other. In the bottom compartment, under the shelves, a pile of sapphires, rubies and diamonds sparkled in the light.

Boris waited for me to say something. Finally I said,

'You won't be able to take all this with you when you escape to the West.'

'Oh yes I shall,' said Boris without the slightest trace of doubt. 'It's all part of my plan.'

'But Galina – does she know about it?'

'Don't worry about Gala, she's all right. Anyway, most of this is hers.'

'Don't tell me any more. I don't want to hear about it!'

Suddenly the idea of Galina Brezhnev defecting wasn't so stupid after all! The doorbell brought a halt to any further discussion. Boris swiftly closed the safe and the wall slid back and the panels re-formed. He hurried to answer the door, and when he came back he was followed by a very beautiful girl wearing some sort of theatrical costume. She looked more suitably dressed for Salome's dance of the seven veils than for a lunch engagement. Boris explained that she was his cousin. Farima, who was appearing at the Romany Theatre that afternoon. 'Farima is the star of the show!' he said proudly. She smiled as Boris introduced her. She had a warm, generous mouth and her small teeth gave her a cheeky smile.

'I am delighted to meet you at last. Boris has told me all about you.'

'Good things, I hope,' I said, following the conventions of such an opening.

'Of course,' she said. 'I'd like very much to get your advice about my act – you know so much about our business . . .'

I was brushing this aside, making the usual remarks, when Boris interrupted: 'Don't you worry, Farima, the maestro will give you good advice and – if you're a good girl – maybe he'll write a song for you. He writes beautiful songs!'

I wondered what he meant by being 'a good girl'. Farima seemed to know. I looked at Boris hoping to see the answer in his face, but once again the doorbell rang.

This time Galina Brezhnev came into the room ahead of Boris. She was carrying a single red rose. With a theatrical geture, she curtseyed before me and handed me the flower. She laughed at my embarrassment and said, 'In Russia women often give flowers to men. It's nothing really unusual. Let's just say it's a mark of respect!' She turned to greet Farima and though it was clear the two women knew each other well, Galina's manner was very superior.

Boris asked Farima to help him serve lunch and they both disappeared into the kitchen. Galina and I sat down at the table. I poured her a gin and tonic, remembering her favourite drink, and got a white wine and mineral water for myself. I lifted my glass to her: '*Na Zdorovye!*' She took a deep swig at her drink and said, 'You should propose that toast for my papa. If anyone needs good health he does. He's not been well lately. He does too much – it's all meetings, conferences, late nights, problems here, there and everywhere. He carries too much on his own shoulders and he is tired, very very tired!' And she downed the rest of the glass in one, I got her another.

When Boris and Farima reappeared they were carrying antique china plates covered with delicious hors d'oeuvres and a bowl of lobster salad. Boris went out and back twice to get champagne, French and Georgian wines. Galina tucked in as though she hadn't eaten for a month. Boris warned us all to leave room for the main course – 'It's called "Beef *à la* Kishinev" – an original gypsy dish. You'll soon see how good it is!' Galina continued as before. Between mouthfuls, she forced more and more wine on Farima. I began to wonder how Farima would ever manage to get on stage that afternoon, but Galina soon solved the problem. Turning to Boris she said, 'You had better ring Marina Stefanovich and tell her to use the understudy. Tell her Farima is indisposed, and if she argues about it, tell her I said so!'

When Galina finally slowed over the first course, Boris and Farima went into the kitchen to bring the main dish. They seemed to be taking a very long time. Galina, who was on her fifth gin, caught my glances towards the kitchen and said quite matter-of-factly: 'The main course will take some time. Boris is fucking FarimA right now.'

TWELVE

Once again I was at a loss for words. I sipped my drink purposefully.

'Oh, I don't mind,' said Galina in the same calm tone. 'It's not his fault. When Farima's had a few, she's anybody's. She can't help it, poor girl.' Galina sighed with what seemed like moral superiority. 'I'm not in the least jealous. He's such a stallion; nobody can tire him. In this case he's just limbering up before the big match . . .'

Galina passed me her glass and I poured her a sixth gin. 'You must be wondering,' she said, the effects of alcohol now quite marked, 'why I, Gala Brezhnev, am so involved with the gypsy boy? Well, the answer is simple, my friend. He's the best fucking lover I have ever had – and I've had a few, I can tell you . . . even though I'm a married woman. Boris is the only one who takes me so I know I've been fucked. And at my age that's important!'

She took another swig of her drink. I was relieved not to be asked to contribute to this conversation. 'And I'm going to hang on to him. I won't let him go. Not bloody likely! I need him. Oh, I know he's a naughty boy. But I have to accept that. I can't find it in me to refuse him anything – just as long as he keeps pleasing me.'

At that moment Boris made a timely reappearance, carrying a steaming joint of beef covered in a red paprika sauce. There was no sign of Farima. Boris carved the meat as though it were a treasured thing, arranging the portions carefully on plates before pouring sauce over them.

Galina added some mixed vegetables to mine and passed it to me. I knew she couldn't keep quiet for long and she didn't: 'And where is dear Farima?'

'Having a little rest,' replied Boris without a flicker. And to me he said, 'You can join her later if you wish.'

It was Galina who answered for me: 'Shut up, Boris! Don't say such stupid things to your guest. Farima wouldn't attract the maestro here, he loves his wife too much.'

I nodded in agreement and the hot sauce burned my throat.

After that we ate in silence for a while. The meat was delicious and if Boris had really cooked it then he had done well. Suddenly Galina whispered something in Boris's ear. I thought for a moment I was going to be left eating the meal all by myself, but only Boris left the room. While he was out, Galina said, 'Do you know, I haven't been able to thank you properly for those two lovely dresses you brought me . . .'

'But you have,' I said.

'Yes, but not your wife. She went to all the trouble of choosing them.'

At that moment Boris returned and put something in Galina's hand. 'Here,' she said, 'please give this to your lovely wife with my thanks,' and she put a beautiful brooch on the table between us. Unlike the jewellery Galina usually wore, this brooch – a small diamond in a delicate setting – was very restrained and elegant.

'It's only a small thing . . . and don't try to refuse it, it's for your wife.'

'Well, at least you must let me bring you something in return . . .'

'God forbid . . .' – her words were now slurred – 'I always like to have the last word, you know . . .'

Her elbow slipped off the table and Boris shot me a glance as if to say, 'You see what I have to put up with?' I frowned at him. Galina would be no exception to the golden rule when dealing with drunks: never assume they won't notice because they always do. She caught the glance, saw my frown and grinned at Boris . . . 'Oh no, my love, I'm not that drunk. Tell Farima to take a shower and go back to bed. You and I will be along later to keep her company.'

Boris looked like a puppy who had been threatened with a spanking, but left the room without protest. When he closed the door behind him, Galina made a great effort to free her mind from the alcohol.

'When do you come back to us again?'

'Probably in the spring or early summer.'

'We will be in Yalta next summer . . . Papa, Mama, the children and me. My husband won't be there – he has to work. I shall make a point of coming to see your show!'

It was a grand announcement, as though it would turn my tour into a Royal Command Performance.

'I'm not sure the tour will take us to Yalta.'

'Oh, it will! I'll see that it does. How much longer are you staying in Moscow now?'

'Another few days. I have some business to attend to, then I'm off.'

Galina stood up, swayed slightly but steadied herself with a hand on the table. 'So, I will see you in the summer.' She kissed me on both cheeks. 'One kiss for you . . . and one for your dear wife.' She then held out her hand to Boris as he came back in. He avoided it, saying, 'I'll just put the maestro in a taxi – I won't be long.'

Once we were safely in the lift, Boris sneered, 'Let them play for a while. Bloody lesbians!' Knowing his tastes, I found the remark rather comical but he had obviously not been slow with the drinks either. He said he would see me at the New Year's Eve party at the

House of Artists, promising we were assured of a wonderful evening. He had arranged for the famous Russian folk singer, Zykina, to be at our table. 'Watch out for her! She has such big balloons you could fly away on them!'

'I'll leave them for you to try.'

'I have! I didn't get far before I crash-landed in her bed!'

Boris was still laughing at his own joke when I got into the taxi and waved him goodbye.

That evening I went downstairs to the hotel restaurant. I still felt quite jaded from the heavy lunch and had decided to have only a light salad. Crossing the foyer I bumped into Sasha, the KGB man who had so nearly ruined Irena's party for Andrei's birthday.

'How nice to see you again,' he said, feigning surprise. 'I was just on my way to have a bite to eat. Why don't you joint me?'

I chose a table beside the fountain – the noise of falling water would upset any recording Sasha might be counting on. The fountain also served another purpose; it acted as a sort of air conditioner in an otherwise very stuffy room. I ordered vodka and herring for Sasha and a salad and Narzan water for myself. The conventions of such a meeting were adhered to and as usual I wondered when the prattle would stop and the real point of the assignation emerge.

I decided to take the initiative. 'Is this a friendly chat, or is it an interrogation?' I suspected Igor Igorovich had sent him.

'Oh, a friendly chat, that's all . . .' he replied, clearly discomposed.

'I'm glad of that,' I said in formal tones, 'because if it isn't I want someone from the British Embassy to be present and a full note to be made of all questions and answers.'

'Oh, it's nothing like that,' said Sasha hastily, 'though I may as well admit that my meeting with you was no accident.'

'There's no need to admit it – I knew it anyway. The KGB are lousy actors.'

Sasha looked even more uncomfortable. 'Actually,' he said, 'it's more a case of wanting to inform you of something . . .'

'Inform me then, I'm listening.'

Sasha leaned forward and spoke very softly. 'I thought it would interest you to know that Boris Buryatsa is at this very moment being interrogated at the offices of Yuri Andropov, Chairman of the KGB . . .'

He waited for this news to take effect, but though my heart nearly stopped I don't think my face gave me away. I did well. Even my voice came out fairly normal. 'By Andropov himself?'

'No, not exactly, but in his office by someone of very high rank.'

He watched me carefully. I pretended to know much more than I did and spoke as though I had intimate knowledge of the Kremlin in-fighting. 'No, of course, it wouldn't be Andropov himself . . . too risky.'

Sasha twitched. I could see him turning over my words in his mind. 'Too risky' – what did that mean? I pressed on: 'There'll be hell to pay over this. Where is Zvigun? He's meant to be looking after Boris.'

It was a dangerous game, but Sasha like a lamb volunteered, 'General Zwigun is away for a few days on a *komandirovka*, a duty visit.'

'So someone thought this was a convenient time. Well, heads will roll when you-know-who hears about it.'

'We're investigating a very serious matter, there's nothing wrong about that,' said Sasha stolidly. His questioning of me had gone awry. 'Any information you could give me would help, however insignificant it you could give me would help, however insignificant itmight appear.' He sounded like a Russian PC Plod.

'Well, what is it all about? I can't help you if I don't know what you think he's done, can I?'

'Murder,' said Sasha smugly, 'well, suspicion of, anyway.'

'Boris! Murder! You must be mad. Boris is no angel, but murder – that's not his style.'

'That remains to be seen,' said Sasha sharply. 'About a year ago a man fell to his death from an express train – a Red Arrow – between Moscow and Leningrad. He was from Finland and everyone thought it was just another drunken Finn. Certainly the post-mortem revealed that the victim had consumed a lot of alcohol. Clearly death from misadventure. End of story you would think. But this time it wasn't.

'A witness came forward. She had been in the next compartment and she said the man had been with two gypsies and that there had been a lot of drinking. The noise had kept her awake for some time. She had finally fallen asleep, but had woken in the middle of the night and heard one of the men say, "Come on, friend, I'll take you to the toilet." Then she heard a door bang and only one man come back . . .'

'So?'

'So that wouldn't have amounted to much, except for one thing. You know about the Finns – you must have come across them many times in Leningrad. Always pissed and always a bloody nuisance – but this one wasn't. This particular Finn was teetotal! He never touched a drop. His wife swears to that, but more importantly, so do other people who knew him here where he was doing engineering work for us. They used to tease him like mad about not drinking, but it made no difference, he wouldn't touch it.'

All I could think of was the Finn who had built Boris's safe for him. Boris had said that he had been drunk and fallen out of a train but that the police had

119

mentioned the possibility of a hit-man, a contract killing . . .

Sasha talked over my thoughts: The theory is now that someone who travelled with the Finn forced a lot of vodka down his throat and then threw him off the train.'

'All right, but what has this to do with Boris Buryatsa?'

'Well,' said Sasha, 'we know that he knew that Finn. He was seen with Comrade Buryatsa at the Bolshoi and even, we believe, visited Buryatsa's apartment. Has he ever said anything to you about him?'

'Why should he? Whenever I talk to Boris it's about general things – the theatre, music – you know he sings very well. We talk about showbusiness, about women – that sort of thing.'

'Not about Finns?'

'Not about Finns!'

Sasha poured himself another vodka and looked as if he were settling in for the night. It suddenly occurred to me that there might indeed be hell to pay if Galina knew about Boris's interrogation, and that perhaps I should try and find a way of getting Sasha to tell her about it. I felt inspired as I said, 'Of course, all this could ruin your career . . .'

He bit hard: 'My career . . . how?'

'Well, look at it this way. Boris Buryatsa is being questioned behind Zvigun's back. And when Zvigun finds out, he's going to know you knew and did nothing about it. And while Brezhnev's still in power that can't be good for you, can it? Or don't you mind waiting until Andropov is the boss? For your reinstatement, I mean.'

'Reinstatement?' The word carried all sorts of dreadful implications and was just what was needed to bring our evening to an abrupt close, Sasha made his excuses and was off, I sat for a while wondering what exactly Sasha would do. It seemed most likely that he would go to Igor Igorovich and let him decide, though he might feel compelled to act by himself.

It was not until much later that I learned that Zvigun had indeed been recalled to Moscow and that Boris had been released amid profuse apologies.

The next evening Boris was waiting for me at the entrance to the House of Artists. My mind flooded with memories as we walked into the building in which my career had been born all those years ago. Very little seemed to have changed since 1940: the large foyer, the wide staircase which splayed out to each side halfway up were exactly the same. Only the music and the people were different. A welcoming party dressed in colourful costumes was singing folk songs as we entered and a glassful of *garelka* – supposedly a Russian peasant drink, but more like liquid fire – was thrust into my hand.

In the main hall the chandeliers sparkled and the tables were laden with splendid Russian delicacies. The place cards bore the names of famous stars from the Bolshoi, the Drama Theatre and at our own table I immediately recognized Zykina, the famous folk singer whose enormous frame dwarfed everyone around her.

It was a glittering occasion. The atmosphere in the hall was marvellous and a happy buzz filled the air. The drink flowed and we toasted everyone and everything we could think of. There were even toasts to people who were despised, particularly KGB personnel.

When the danceband took over from the balalaikas the floor began to fill with couples. I jumped to my feet and with a kiss on Zykina's hand, asked her to dance. A true performer, she grabbed a red rose from one of the flower bowls and put it between her teeth. She was Carmen, all fifteen stone of her. We pirouetted and tangoed and waltzed around the dance floor and as the band played the final notes Zykina picked me up like a baby and spun me round in her arms. This brought a standing ovation from the crowd and flowers were flung from all directions.

I was to look back on that evening as one of the most enjoyable in all the time spent in Russia.

THIRTEEN

Later that spring I was back with another tour. This tour was memorable not only because of the outstanding success we had in Moscow, Kiev, Leningrad, Tashkent and Baku, but because this was when Boris first put his foreign-marriage plan into operation.

The lucky girl was Isla St Clair, who at the time was hardly known in Britain but enjoyed great popularity in Russia. She was a young vivacious Scots girl, very easy to work with and always full of energy and good cheer. Her only failing – if it can be so described – was that she fell in love too easily, each time more passionately than the time before and each time with someone destined to be the love of her life. Even though her romantic dreams were invariably shattered, she didn't remain depressed for long and usually bounced back to reality until the next contender came along.

Boris naturally made her his prime target. He did everything to try and impress her but all his efforts were in vain. He couldn't understand it, and asked me to intercede and persuade Isla to marry him just so that he could get out of Russia. But Isla was much too much of a romantic to fall in with his plans. At the time she had given her heart to a young Russian singer called Grisha and, as usual, this was the man of her dreams. She wanted no part in a marriage of convenience, however temporary.

For Boris another attempt to leave Russia had gone

sour. He regarded it as only a set-back, however, and seemed just as determined to get out as ever. There was also something different about him: he seemed less aggressive than before, more self-assured somehow, and with Galina he was even more acquiescent, even more her puppy-dog.

This new-look Boris had nothing to do with his KGB interrogation. He had emerged from that unscathed and unchastened, only to plunge even deeper into the criminal underworld. The word was that Boris was now one of the bosses of a smuggling ring bringing goods in across the Soviet border. When I heard that, I thought how ridiculous were all his marrying plans: if he could smuggle goods into Russia, surely it wouldn't be too difficult to smuggle himself out?

But perhaps that was the real plan. Certainly Boris's need grew more urgent every day. Leonid Brezhnev was very ill and getting worse. It was reputedly more his own determination than all the medical skill lavished on him which kept him alive. Many players in the political theatre knew what was going on and were merely waiting for his last gasp to summon them on stage.

Andropov was at the head of the queue, of course. With his long experience as boss of the KGB, he was the strongest candidate for the major role and was impatient to take it. Although the Russian propaganda machine concealed Brezhnev's deteriorating condition from the masses, Andropov's accession was much feared in certain quarters. He had access to all the KGB files and many feared that his assumption of power would mean that some files would be closed – permanently.

Boris must have known that his days were numbered, yet he seemed on the surface to have no more cares than usual. I wondered whether his calm exterior came from the knowledge that both he and Galina could escape when the time was right as packages on their own smuggling runs. Even as I wondered, Leonid Brezhnev, defying the laws of probability and medical science, made what appeared to be a convincing recovery.

I was back in Moscow in January 1977 – but only so that I could escort Aram Khatchaturian on his long-awaited visit to London. I had organized a great deal of publicity for the composer and had gone to endless trouble to make sure that arrangements went smoothly. I had contacted everyone I knew in Fleet Street and in television to make sure that they all knew the day and time of his arrival at Heathrow. January is not the best time for concerts and I needed plenty of press coverage to sell concert tickets so soon after Christmas.

Unfortunately, the Russian bureaucratic machine completely ruined all my careful preparation. Everything had been arranged for Khatchaturian to leave with his family on the Saturday, but at the last moment it was discovered that the exit visas had not been signed. The visas were awaiting us in the Soviet Ministry of Foreign Affairs, but were useless without a signature. We missed our planned flight and did not arrive at Heathrow until the next day, by which time the press coverage had been lost.

Despite this inauspicious start the concerts were a huge success and acclaimed by the critics. The media began to cover his every move and Khatchaturian was delighted with the whole visit. 'When I get on to the rostrum in the Albert Hall or the Festival Hall,' he said, 'I feel on top of the world. London is the Mecca of music and culture!' And London certainly made him welcome.

My tours to the Soviet Union now took place on a regular basis. Gosconcert seemed more and more enthusiastic and I tried always to find new acts and new performers to take on each tour. For many months

I scarcely saw Boris at all and was beginning to think that he had disappeared from my life. But in 1978, a few days after we had arrived in Leningrad, Boris booked into the Hotel Europa where we were staying. I suspected from his flamboyant dress that he was after the foreign girls again and I was soon proved right. There were a number of girls in the dance team but once again Boris failed to find a bride. They all told him they had left their boyfriends or fiancés behind in London, but I knew the real reason was that they had been warned off by Natasha, our interpreter.

Natasha was a drinking chum of Galina's and I could guess what kind of stories she was telling the girls about Boris. Perhaps she was just protecting Galina's interests, but whatever her motives she certainly dissuaded the girls from becoming involved.

This series of failures upset him, and it wasn't long before he appeared at my room looking very miserable. We had breakfast together and I tried to cheer him up, but when I asked him about Brezhnev's health he became even more downcast.

'You know how much the old man is my lifeline. God knows how much longer he will live. When he goes, I'm doomed – I know that. That's part of the reason why I'm here. When I heard that you had a load of girls with you, I thought I'd try the marriage scheme again. But I can't seem to get anywhere with them. I'll have to try a different way. And I don't think I've got much time, the old man is up and down from one day to the next.'

'Do you have another plan?'

'I'm sorry, my friend, I'm not telling. I know you'll wish me well, but this one is too dangerous to share with anyone!'

I was greatly relieved to hear this and tried to change the subject by asking after Galina. For some reason this seemed to alert him to the danger of bugs. He put his finger to his lips and led the way out into the corridor. Did the KGB never bug corridors, I wondered?

Boris kept his voice low: 'Things have been happening since I saw you last. They're getting ready to pounce and I'm only keeping them off my back by bribing everyone around me.'

'But what about Galina? Surely she protects you?'

'Oh yes,' said Boris sarcastically. 'If only I could rely on that – but when the ship starts to sink even the rats jump off.'

'What do you mean? What's wrong?'

'Plenty,' he said grimly. 'There's that bastard Zvigun for a start – you know, Gala's uncle. I have to play "One Way Street" with him practically every night.'

'One Way Street?'

'It's a game with only one rule. And that is when I win he gives me an IOU and when he wins I must give him cash. That way he can never lose.'

'Have you told Galina?'

'Of course, but she arranged for him to protect me. He's her favourite uncle and she tells me not to grumble about a few lousy roubles and to think how lucky I am to have the protection of the Deputy Chairman of the KGB. Protection! It's costing me a fortune and the stakes in the game keep going up. He's started dropping hints about projects he thinks I should put my money into. They're all connected with some sort of game he's playing with Andropov – they're fighting each other all the time. He is even feeding his brother-in-law, the mighty Brezhnev, with all sorts of stories to get some special favours in return . . . I tell you, Zvigun is dangerous. He's got a foul temper, he's rude and rough and he'll not give an inch to anybody. A typical primitive bloody peasant.'

And you're a primitive Russian gypsy, I thought, and that makes the two of you really dangerous. I wondered where Yuri Churbanov, Galina's husband, fitted into all this. He surely felt betrayed and humiliated by his wife and the fact that the whole of Russia knew that her favourite lover was a gypsy must have made matters worse. Churbanov, I thought, must also be part of this deadly game, must also be waiting in the wings for his moment to pounce.

We left Leningrad at the end of that week for Yalta, where we were to stay for three weeks. We had a heavy schedule of concerts but were being given a few free days so that we could enjoy the Black Sea and the wonderful Crimean climate – an unheard-of gesture by Gosconcert.

Our hotel was close to the beach and our rooms were on the sixth floor. The hotel was quite luxurious by Russian standards and didn't have that all-too-familiar run-down look and feel. From our windows we had breathtaking views out over the sea and across to the nearby mountains. Almost hidden in the greenery of the mountain slopes were the villas belonging to the Soviet élite. It was here that Leonid Brezhnev spent his summer holidays and the guards on duty around the grounds did not attempt to hide their existence. Brezhnev was in residence at the time and the poor state of his health meant that there were hordes of doctors and medical staff constantly coming and going from the building. I was conscious of how many lives lay in the hands of his doctors and I wondered if they guessed how many people prayed for them to keep Brezhnev alive.

The Sunday after we arrived I was sitting on a bench outside the stage door enjoying the sunshine and the view over the sea. Most of the performers were also outside, relaxing before the matinée performance. What had been a quiet Sunday afternoon all of a sudden turned into something very different. Groups of civilian police seemed to appear from nowhere, and dog handlers with massive dogs on the end of chains circled the building. I told everyone to get inside the building, but delayed at the door myself. Through a crack I caught a glimpse of a big black car with tinted windows stopping before the door leading to the VIP box. I didn't have time to see any more. A man with an Alsatian walked towards my door and banged it shut from the outside.

The first bell rang and the audience started to take their seats. The auditorium was so full of KGB that I wondered if Brezhnev himself had decided to pay us a visit. At that moment Andrei Pavlovich, the theatre director, appeared and whispered urgently, 'Come, come, someone wants to meet you!' I walked with him to the VIP box where Galina, a half-empty glass already in her hand, greeted me very formally. The people around her stood back at a respectful distance as she introduced her son, who enthused for a few minutes about the English pop-music scene.

When the second bell went I made to leave and Galina asked me to return and have a drink at the interval. 'With pleasure, Madame,' I said, and kissed her hand. When we left the box Andrei Pavlovich said, 'I'd no idea you knew Galina Brezhnev so well!' but his tone was admiring, not suspicious. I got on well with Andrei. On a previous visit to Yalta I discovered that he had been stationed in Poland during the war. He spoke Polish quite well and loved to practise it on me.

After the first half Andrei seemed almost proud as he led me into the VIP box. Galina stepped forward, complimenting me on the show, which she said she had greatly enjoyed. She then introduced me to the man standing next to her: 'This is my husband, Yuri, the Deputy Minister of Internal Affairs.'

'Of course,' I said, quite taken aback, and we shook hands, exchanging the usual courtesies, after which he surprised me by saying, 'Actually I've known about you for some time. We have a mutual friend – Vsevolod Malinsky. He told me what a pleasant association the two of you had in London.'

It was not a good name to be linked with as far as I

was concerned: Malinsky was one of the Russians that Lord Home threw out of Britain during a big clean-up of Soviet diplomats in London. But I had known nothing about the spying side of his affairs; he had been helpful with the arrangements for my tours, that was all. The first I had known about his other activities had been when I read about it in the newspapers. So to Galina's husband I was studiously non-committal about Malinsky.

Churbanov then went on to talk about the show and the quality of the performance. 'We're grateful to you for bringing us such a variety of talent. But I understand that you yourself like gypsy music much more than anything else. Am I right?' He stressed the word 'gypsy' and I hesitated. But Galina cut right in, interrupting rudely, and asked me to join her and get her a drink. We left her husband looking embarrassed, which seemed to please Galina. 'He's so jealous,' she said when we were out of earshot. 'And how is your dear wife?' she asked in a louder tone.

'Very well,' I said.

'You know, I've heard so much about her, I really must meet her one day.'

'That would be very nice, Madame.'

'Please – Galina.'

'Not in front of all these people here.'

She studied me very closely, looking hard into my eyes. 'Perhaps you're right. I think you are a clever man. Discretion is a virtue. Papa is always saying that. By the way, I'm sorry he's not here. He wanted to come, but something came up unexpectedly. It's a pity. He would have enjoyed it – particularly the dancing girls!'

The second bell rang. I started to move away, but Galina took hold of my hand. The soft voice was back as she asked, 'Have you seen Boris lately?'

'Not since I was in Moscow.'

'You haven't seen him in Yalta?' There was surprise in her voice.

'Is he here? I didn't know.'

She looked really puzzled, but covered up quickly. 'I know he was going to the Crimea – I just assumed he meant Yalta. Perhaps he's somewhere else – after all, the Crimea's a big place, isn't it?' She turned it into a joke and both of us laughed quite falsely . . .

In fact, though I didn't know it at the time, Boris was indeed on the shores of the Black Sea, but he was closer to the Turkish border, at Batumi, some 450 miles away. Boris wasn't in Batumi in search of a suntan. It had taken him a long time, but he had finally found what he thought was the way out of Russia. And the mere fact that Galina had asked me where Boris was was clear proof that this time she was not in on his plan.

Boris had made contact with Ahmed Fakriz, a notorious Turkish smuggler, a member of the Turkish 'Mafia' and a known killer. Fakriz did not normally deal with outsiders like Boris, but Boris had made sure that the Turk's greed was well and truly roused. He proposed that gold and diamonds would be brought as close as possible to the Russian–Turkish border and that these would be swapped for Western goods normally unobtainable in Russia to be supplied by Fakriz and his men. Boris made it a condition that part of the value of the gold and diamonds be deposited in foreign currency, not roubles, in a bank in Istanbul in his name.

This apparently worried Fakriz a great deal, not because it was a difficult thing to do, but because he wasn't sure what Boris intended to do with the money in the account. Boris should have told him that he intended it as a nest egg for use after his escape, but he didn't. He wanted Fakriz to think of their smuggling arrangement as a long-term deal. If Fakriz had known it was just a single operation there was no reason why he shouldn't double-cross Boris and make off with the gold and diamonds. Fakriz did not trust Boris and Boris did not trust Fakriz. This mistrust was the reason for Boris's trip to Batumi. Fakriz had asked for a face-to-face meeting to iron out any problems between them. Boris had agreed, as he too wanted to see the man who was going to provide him with his escape route out of Russia.

Fakriz had suggested that the meeting take place on his yacht, a floating cocktail cabinet of a boat, much loved by millionaire sailors. He would play the innocent rich Turkish holidaymaker, cruising around the Black Sea, and Boris would join him aboard when he got close to Russian waters. The meeting was first arranged to take place at night, but then Fakriz unexpectedly changed it to daytime. Boris had protested. It would be difficult enough to board Fakriz's yacht at night without arousing suspicion; in the daytime it would be suicidal. But Fakriz, as though testing his new partner, insisted.

In the end Boris simply rowed out to the boat as if he was a holidaymaker wanting to have a look at a big yacht, and then climbed aboard. It made me wonder why on earth Boris had gone to such extremes with all his plans to escape when apparently all that was necessary was to row out of Russia on a sunny afternoon! I discovered later that Boris had bribed a KGB official to ensure his freedom of movement in Batumi. What Boris did not know was that the bribe amounted to another nail in his coffin; the KGB man had only pretended to take the bribe and although Boris's activities were not interfered with, they were carefully monitored.

I was also given a detailed account of the conversation between the two men on board the yacht. Fakriz apparently didn't even get up from his chair where he sat drinking coffee as Boris climbed the ladder to the deck of the yacht. He merely motioned Boris to a seat next to him. They sat in silence for a while, sizing each other up. Then Boris helped himself to a large brandy from the array of bottles on the table. A steward moved forward to help but Fakriz waved him away.

It was Fakriz who spoke first: 'It wasn't difficult, was it?'

'Not at all,' said Boris. For some minutes they discussed landing points and rendezvous, nothing that justified such a risky meeting. Finally, Boris said, 'Are you satisfied with the arrangements?'

'I am,' said Fakriz. 'It is a simple bargain: you deliver the diamonds and I pay part in goods and part in cash into your bank account.'

'The bank account – is that a problem?'

'Not at all,' said Fakriz. 'You simply tell me now what name you want it in, and give me a couple of specimen signatures and that's it.' Then he grinned and said, 'I suppose you won't want the bank statements sent to your home address!'

Boris laughed. All his fears about Fakriz were melting away. With such a man as an ally, he could make a fortune. No need to escape yet – he could wait until the Istanbul account was really fat.

I heard nothing more from Galina, or from Boris for that matter, during the rest of our stay in Yalta. But I wasn't lulled into a false sense of security. One morning when I was playing chess in a small square just off the promenade, I heard a voice behind me: 'Good move, Maestro, you are playing like a real Russian!' I turned round to find a young man with bushy red hair. He continued to chat during my game and afterwards we went for a drink in a nearby bar. He introduced himself to me as Kremerov. His name didn't mean anything to me, but I noticed that the bartender ignored the long queue and served us first. Kremerov turned out to be one of the most popular character actors in the Soviet Union and also a highly acclaimed film star. After our drink we strolled together in the direction of my hotel.

'Do they know anything about me in your country?' he asked. I had to confess that they didn't and he was quite upset.

'But my films were shown at Cannes . . .'

I told him that that really didn't mean very much. Soviet films didn't get much of a showing in England, so he would have to forgive our ignorance. As I told him this, I looked up to a higher level of the promenade and had the immediate sense of being watched. The young couple who walked hand in hand seemed to be trying too hard to look as though they were in love. Kremerov followed my eyes and obviously had the same thought. He beckoned me to a steel barrier overlooking the beach and, as we leant on it and looked out to sea, he reminded me suddenly of Boris at one of our first meetings. In the same tense secretive tone he said, 'Here I am a star, but I'd like to expand my talents in some other parts of the world . . .'

'What do you mean?' I asked, as if I didn't know.

'Well, if you could see your way to taking some of my clips to London and perhaps being my sponsor . . .'

I stopped him there. I said I would be pleased to take some of his work and show it to people in the West, but that was all I could do. When I looked up the young couple had been joined by an older man. They looked out over our heads to the horizon. There was absolutely no doubt; we were being observed.

That night I was introduced in the theatre to the General Director of the Crimea Philharmonia, Nicolai Yurevich Gasparov, a war hero and personal friend of Leonid Brezhnev since childhood. Nicolai Yurevich was studiously polite. He thanked me for my concerts in Yalta and invited all of us to a farewell lunch in Semfiropol, the airport from which we would leave the Crimea.

True to his word, lunch was arranged at the Intourist hotel in Semfiropol. Afterwards the director asked me to leave the table and took me into a room which looked like the hastily vacated office of the hotel manager. He pointed to a chair and I sat. 'I'll skip all the usual overtures,' he said, 'and come straight to the point. I know all about your experiences in our country and I assure you that you are always a welcome visitor here, but some things have changed since the war . . . one can't expect you to know about our laws these days.' He looked quite affable when he spoke, but it sounded sinister.

'What do you mean? Has one of us done something against the law?'

'I don't think so . . . well, that is, not yet – but it is always as well to be cautious in these matters. It is my duty to clear up any doubts . . .' He seemed to be rambling, which unnerved me.

I was blunter than I intended: 'What's all this about?'

'Since you ask,' he said, not looking at me, but apparently studying his fingertips intently, 'I will tell you. You have been seen in conversation with the actor Kremerov. I'm sure that this was simply professional chat, shop talk, but people like him do tend to involve others in their private affairs. Do try to understand I am responsible for everything that happens, so to speak, under my roof – that of the Semfiropol Philharmonia – and such talk could be unhealthy for you . . .'

'What are you saying – that I shouldn't speak to Soviet film stars?'

'Not exactly, but Kremerov has tried it before and he will try it again. Whenever he gets a chance, he seeks friends in the West. We think he is looking for someone to help him to defect. And we would not like that someone to be you. He was due to stay for another two weeks in Yalta, but he has been asked to cut short his holiday. I didn't want any trouble.'

'Thank you, Nicolai Yurevich,' I said through clenched teeth, 'thank you for enlightening me. I am quite sure that I will not be hearing from Kremerov any more.'

At the end of August 1979, I returned to Russia, this time to arrange the appearance of Volodya Vasiliev and Katya Maximova at the Royal Command Performance in November that year. It was the first time a Soviet act had been included in the show. The Soviet authorities were initially reluctant to allow the dancers to take part, on the grounds that they disapproved of organized charities, but in the end they agreed.

Vasiliev and Maximova danced before the Queen, who was obviously delighted, as was the audience, who gave the couple a standing ovation. Sadly, these dancers were the only two to have the honour. Within a short time the world was suddenly shocked and angered by the Red Army's invasion of Afghanistan.

FOURTEEN

My next tour was with the New Seekers. The officials at Gosconcert, delighted that I had decided to fulfil the contract despite the political difficulties following Afghanistan, rewarded us with a comfortable big-city-only tour of Moscow, Leningrad, Riga, Tallin and Baku. The welcome of the audiences was greater than ever and we had the unusual experience of people shaking our hands on the street and thanking us for coming to the Soviet Union 'in such difficult times'.

Before we left Moscow Boris turned up at my hotel room and as usual beckoned me into the corridor. I told him I thought the KGB probably had enough to do now without bugging the poor Westerners, but Boris joked that there were so few tourists that I was the only one worth bugging! He started apologizing for not having seen me for so long – somehow we must have missed one another . . . it was as much my fault as his . . . his work had taken up all his time. I tried to imagine what he would do if I told him all I now knew about his links with the Turkish Mafia.

Eventually he said: 'I've got a message for you which I wanted to deliver before you leave Moscow tomorrow.' Not for the first time I wondered who kept Boris so accurately informed of my movements. 'I promised Gala that I would give you a personal message from her. She asked me to thank you on her behalf for coming to the Soviet Union with your artistes – in spite of the political developments.'

'Tell her,' I said, as though we were two superpowers exchanging diplomatic notes, 'tell her that I appreciate her gratitude and I will continue with my visits as usual.'

'I'll tell her,' he said, failing to see the comic aspect. 'I expect to see her soon. She was very busy for a while and away from Moscow – she even started to have an affair with a young major in the air force, but she soon came back to me.' He grinned in a wolfish way and added, after a pause, 'She was disappointed with his performance at ground level.' As usual he laughed loudly at his own joke.

'I'm glad things are going well for you, Boris. You seem happier.'

'I am. You'll be delighted to know I am very close to a solution at last. I daren't say more.'

I was relieved, and then embarrassed because Boris went on to thank me for all I had done for him. 'You see how I've taken your advice: I dress more modestly now and try to blend in with the general scene. I don't provoke the Beast any more than necessary. You were right. I was getting above myself. But my time is coming, believe me! Then you'll see how splendid I can be!'

I felt quite sorry for him. Here he was dreaming of freedom – and wealth – outside Russia, and all the time the KGB were playing him along with an informer right inside his gang.

After an extremely successful tour, we arrived back in Moscow to give our final three performances. Boris appeared backstage one night and he brought with him a young army officer whom he introduced to me as Captain Yuri Nikolayevich Mozarin. The number of decorations on his uniform suggested that he had already had a distinguished career. Boris made a great fuss of him, so much so that I began to wonder if

Mozarin was his boyfriend.

It soon became clear that I was mistaken. Captain Mozarin went after the women in the show like a hound in full cry. I asked Boris where they had met and he told me that Zvigun had brought the captain along to one of their card games. I asked which department in the army was favoured with the captain's presence. 'He's in the KGB,' said Boris without a flicker. He grinned at my reaction and added, 'Don't worry, Stanley. He may be in the KGB but his real interest is in women and gambling!' I felt sure from the way he spoke that Mozarin also shared Galina's bed.

Later I heard from another contact that young Captain Mozarin was not all he seemed. 'There isn't a more fanatical, dedicated policeman in the whole of the KGB,' he said. It was another piece of information that I filed away in that section of my brain marked 'Not for Boris'.

It was around the same time that I learned that the KGB operation against Boris and the smugglers had not gone well. Ahmed Fakriz had found out about the KGB plant and a man called Oleg Torski had been given the cement-boot treatment. His body, held down by a concrete base around his ankles, had been found floating upright in shallow water off a Turkish beach. At first the KGB suspected Boris, or his brother Sima, but though they had called them both in for questioning, they had got nowhere. Boris had merely mentioned Galina's name, and a telephone call from the Ministry of the Interior had ordered their release. The call had apparently come from Yuri Churbanov himself.

Although one KGB plant had been disposed of, Boris and Ahmed were in the process of acquiring another. The more I heard about Yuri Mozarin the more he seemed to be every inch a policeman, a born KGB operator, and when tales started to circulate in Moscow society that he was going downhill and associating with all the wrong people, gambling and womanizing and drinking too much, I felt even surer that Boris was in serious trouble.

My suspicions were well founded. Captain Yuri Mozarin had in fact been placed in charge of the operation against Boris and his gang. His brief was to win over Boris's confidence by falling in with his life-style and placing himself under obligation to Boris. He played his role of deception with great finesse, allowing Boris to pick up his gambling debts and shower him with expensive gifts. At the same time he fed Boris with false information designed to make him feel more secure.

The intelligence reports continued to come in from the Crimea. Mozarin was sure that in the end he would be able to link the gypsy with Fakriz: it was just a question of waiting till Boris implicated himself or asked directly for Mozarin's help. In the meantime Mozarin issued orders to his counterparts in Batumi that no one was to interfere with the movements of the yacht.

Boris for his part was well pleased with the captain, believing his recruit to be shaping up well. He took him to parties, theatres, and often let him win at cards. He had also bailed him out of difficult situations, even paying for a private abortion for one of Mozarin's girlfriends and a great deal more in hush money besides.

Mozarin had now accepted so much money and so many gifts that Boris felt very sure of himself. So sure that one evening after he had once again cleared Mozarin's gambling debts he asked him 'to use his influence'. It was what Mozarin had been waiting for. Boris told Mozarin of his 'old friend' from Turkey who often came in his yacht to fish the waters round Batumi. Boris wanted to be able to see him without difficulty or obstruction from the local authorities. He also wanted his brother Sima to be able to deliver a valuable gift to his friend in Batumi and to be assured of a safe passage. Mozarin was happy to oblige and both men, having got what they wanted, shook hands.

Boris's preoccupation with worries about Brezhnev's health may have clouded his judgement of Mozarin and made him less cautious. Certainly he was becoming increasingly desperate to leave and, as I discovered later, was planning his last deal with Fakriz, which was to have been his passage to freedom. Galina had only added to his worries and feelings of desperation, as I discovered next time I saw Boris.

He arrived late in the evening at my hotel and was rather the worse for wear, which was unusual. He lay back in a chair proposing nonsensical toasts from a bottle of vodka. The more he drank the more sober and depressed he seemed to become.

He had spent the earlier part of the evening with Galina, who had rung him up in the middle of a card game. She sounded depressed and said she wanted a party to cheer her up. Boris didn't need telling what sort of party she wanted. He made several phonecalls and then told his guests – they included Zvigun, Kolevatov, the chief of Moscow's State Circus, and Nikolai Shcholokov, the Minister of Internal Affairs – that the game had to be disbanded. Shortly after the gamblers left Boris opened the door to three couples – and then to Galina. He spared me no details in describing the sex orgy that followed. The women had competed to see who could raise the biggest erection – he said Galina and he had won – before all the participants connected themselves to one another so as to form one great copulating ring around the room.

When that was over and everyone was tired, Boris and Galina had retired to the master bedroom. Boris asked Galina why she had been so depressed earlier. Before answering she poured two large glasses of gin with a little tonic in each. She had handed one to Boris before lying down beside him.

He told me how she had begun to stroke his hair, saying: 'We are two of a kind, you and I, Boris. You know me and I know you just as well. Is it any wonder I was depressed? I had a terrible row with Yuri – he had another fit of jealousy – and then I went to see Papa who looked terrible. He's getting worse every day. He keeps feeling giddy and he can't keep his balance. He used to be such a strong man. Now Andropov more or less does what he likes without even asking Father's approval. If it goes on like this, soon they'll just ignore the fact that he's still alive!'

'Surely they wouldn't dare!' Boris had protested.

'I'm not so sure about that.' Boris had tried to cheer her up but she had gone on speculating about their joint fate after her father's death. It wasn't herself she was worried about, she had said, it was Boris. She had then burst into tears and declared her love for him and vowed that she would see that no harm came to him. Tired of her histrionics Boris asked her how she could possibly protect him. At that she had stopped crying and had drawn herself up against the pillow . . .

'I am Leonid Brezhnev's daughter and they will do as I say!'

In 1980 relations between the West and Russia reached a new low. There was the boycott of the Olympic Games, the severing of cultural relations with the United States, and political attacks on the Soviets from every country except the satellite states in the East.

Brezhnev's health was now deteriorating so fast that even the man in the street was aware that he was very ill. In the West there was open speculation about who his successor would be. In fact he was already in power, even if he did not occupy the top seat just yet. It was not for nothing that he was head of the KGB; he had masterminded the take-over for a long time. He had started to forge a steel ring around the country and the links in the chain were his KGB officers.

Every now and then Leonid Brezhnev would appear to be on the mend and he would then make vigorous decisions and cancel some of Andropov's edicts. But such rallies did not last long and it was clear that the old lion was on his way out. Boris and Galina, like the rest of the Brezhnev clique, were forced to lie low. The parties were still held, but more discreetly. The Brezhnev people for the most part followed that old adage: when the wolf is on the prowl, find a big tree!

They broke that rule just before Christmas in 1981. And it was to be their undoing. It had been decided to hold a Festival of the Soviet Circus. The gala performance was to be attended by all the stars of showbusiness and distinguished friends of the circus. The combination of the circus and a society night out was too much for Galina and her friends to resist. The fact that the invitation arrived during one of her father's remissions – he even considered going himself – made her determined to show them who was boss.

She chose her entourage carefully, and on the night of the gala she made her entrance accompanied by the wife of circus chief Kolevatov, actress Larissa Pashkova and the wife of Internal Affairs Minister Shcholokov, all of them displaying their magnificent jewellery. But Galina, with her priceless show of diamonds, upstaged everyone – everyone that is until Irina Bugrimova, the circus lion tamer, arrived. Rumours that Irina had the finest private gem collection in Russia were confirmed that evening for all to see. Galina was furious and left the party abruptly in a fit of unconcealed pique.

Galina later told Boris of her humiliation and Boris foolishly – perhaps out of greed, perhaps out of misplaced affection – took steps to ensure that it would not happen again. On 31 December that year, just when all Russia was preparing for the New Year celebrations,

Irina Bugrimova was robbed of her whole collection.

Early in 1982 when I was once again back in Moscow everyone was talking about the theft of the Bugrimova jewels. It did not take long for suspicion to fall on Boris. Whether this was because he had been careless at the scene of the crime or whether Yuri Churbanov had seen this as a perfect opportunity to nail his wife's lover and had planted the thought in the examining magistrate's mind, no one seemed able to decide. But one thing was certain: when the time came for the interrogation Boris put on his best mink coat and mink-lined boots and drove in his Mercedes to Lefortovo Prison. He didn't come out that day or the next; on the third day he was transferred to the Lubyanka.

FIFTEEN

What they did to Boris Buryatsa in the Lubyanka one can only shudder to think. But he must have talked his head off. The whole Turkish smuggling operation was wiped out in one night. It was Mozarin who led the team which snatched Sima while he was on his way to a rendezvous on Ahmed Fakriz's yacht, and it was Mozarin who took Sima's place and rowed out alone to the yacht, which was just inside Turkish waters off Batumi.

Waiting close by in the darkness were fast boats containing boarding parties of KGB men armed with the new Kalashnikov automatics. Sima was to have carried a small satchel full of diamonds and other stones. As he swung up the lowered companionway, Yuri Mozarin – who was not unlike Sima in build – kept his hat well down to shield his face, but made sure the satchel was clearly visible.

Fakriz was the first to spot that the man on his deck was not Sima, but by then it was too late. Mozarin fired the shot which was to call in the boarding parties – not in the air as he had intended, but between the eyes of Ahmed Fakriz as he went for his gun. That was the only shot that was needed. Once his men were aboard, Mozarin brought the yacht into Russian waters and the haul of goods and drugs which were on her made the triumph extra-sweet. Captain Mozarin became Major Mozarin that very night.

He had played his part well during his infiltration of Boris's operations. So well that when Boris was first questioned – about the Bugrimova robbery – and was asked if he wished anyone informed of his detention, he named Galina Brezhnev first, and Captain Mozarin second. Poor Boris really believed that he had corrupted the captain so well that he would defend him against the might of the rest of the KGB.

Galina Brezhnev let him down, too. Whether she just threw him to the wolves because she had found out he intended to leave Russia without her, or whether she was genuinely unable to help him, is unclear. What is certain is that Andropov felt confident enough to move against a great number of people – something he would never have dared to do when Brezhnev was a fit man. Irena told me that Galina was completely out of touch with what was happening, because Foreign Minister Andrei Gromyko had taken her in for 'special work' on the archives of his ministry and away from any contact with her friends.

Her friends were in any case becoming thin on the ground. Andropov's men arrested the circus boss Kolevatov and also Yuri Sokolov of 'Yeliseyevski' delicatessen fame, who had a million roubles' worth of antique jewellery that he seemed unable to account for when the KGB called at his apartment. And there were more arrests to come. It was not a good time to be a Brezhnev supporter.

And then I heard the most shocking thing of all: Boris had committed suicide in the Lubyanka. He had been found hanging from a beam in his cell. There were those who thought that it was murder, not suicide – and they may very well have been right; it certainly would not have been the first time that the KGB had carried out executions before a trial.

I was due to go back to London the next evening but I was so distressed that I can't even remember what I did for most of that day. Had I let Boris down? Should I have done more? Fear also played a part. What had Boris told them of me? I ran through all the warnings I had received from various people, and how I had ignored most of them. Had Boris told them about the presents he had given me – or those Galina had given me?

These thoughts occupied my mind as I walked to the offices of Gosconcert to have the normal pre-departure meeting with Igor Igorovich to discuss possible future tours. As I was ushered into Igor's office I was dismayed to see Mozarin sitting behind the desk. Igor Igorovich jumped to his feet uneasily and introduced me to Major Yuri Mozarin. We shook hands and made the conventional remarks about having met before, which gave the major his opening.

'Ah yes, it was Boris Buryatsa who introduced me to you, wasn't it?'

'Indeed it was, Major.' The words almost choked me. It was a trap, surely it was a trap. Igor Igorovich got up and left the room.

'Boris has told me a great deal about you . . . he is a great fan of yours.'

'*Was*.'

'What do you mean?' The ingratiating smile disappeared.

'Don't play games, Major. The whole world knows Boris is dead. And if we are to continue with this conversation I insist on having a British Embassy official present.'

'My dear Mr Laudan . . .' he fawned, but the meeting was effectively at an end. He tried several other openers, including my connection with Galina Brezhnev, whether my travels had taken me to Batumi, if I knew Sima. But he never recovered his hold on the questioning and I felt confident enough to stand up and make my way towards the door.

As I reached for the handle, the door opened and there was Igor Igorovich, looking nervous. Even if he hadn't been listening, he couldn't have failed to note the tension in the air. 'I hope you two had a nice chat,' he said, his words falling to the floor with an almost audible thud. He tried again with, 'Well, I'm sure you will be good friends. We at Gosconcert are very fond of Mr Laudan.' And suiting the action to the words, he kissed me on both cheeks. Mozarin in his turn stuck out his hand. I shook it and said firmly, 'Goodbye, Major,' I hoped that goodbye would be for ever.

Leonid Brezhnev died in early November 1982 and on the fifteenth of that month millions of people watched his funeral on television. The world saw the Judas kiss of Andropov as he moved slowly towards Galina and expressed his condolences to her in her 'sad loss'. The world also saw the two men who followed Galina at the funeral, though few would realize that they were not her bodyguards but KGB guards. Andropov was now in power and Galina was to be placed in a rehabilitation centre, the official reason being that she was mentally disturbed, driven by greed, an addiction to alcohol and a gross sexual appetite.

Andropov went wild for just fifteen months before he too died. While he lived the Brezhnev 'clan' was cut down. Zvigun took cyanide. Sokolov was shot by firing squad. Kolevatov got a thirteen-year prison sentence. Minister Shcholokov was discharged from his post and removed from the Central Committee for 'mistakes he allowed to happen in his ministry'. His wife feared that worse was to come and she killed herself by jumping out of their apartment window.

After Andropov died, the new General Secretary, Konstantin Chernenko, tried to undo some of Andropov's excesses towards the Brezhnevs. Leonid Brezhnev had looked after him and he now tried to do his best to repay that debt. The investigation of Shcholokov was dropped and he was given a post in the Defence Ministry. Galina was released and actually appeared at the Kremlin celebrations of International Women's Day in March of 1984.

After Chernenko became ill the KGB moved back in. Shcholokov was their first victim. They stripped him of his rank as a general in the army, then they announced that they were reopening the Andropov investigation. When he heard that he put on his dress uniform with all his decorations and medals, loaded his hunting rifle and, putting the muzzle in his mouth, shot himself through the head. That was on 13 December 1984.

Three months later Chernenko died and it was open season on the Brezhnevs once again. Galina went back under house arrest.

By then I was well out of it. After the Mozarin business Rosa had been appointed chief interpreter and administrator, and it was she who unwittingly convinced me that I should discontinue my trips to the Soviet Union. She mentioned the name almost casually, too casually for my liking, but then she was never a great actress.

'Do you remember someone called Rubinzik?' My heart practically stopped.

'Rubinzik? No, I don't think so. Which tour was that on?'

'No, not recently. A long time ago. During the war?'

'I don't think so – why?'

'Oh, it's just that my husband is working with someone called Rubinzik and his father said he knew you from the war times . . .'

'You met so many people in the war,' I said, as though trying to remember. 'What did he do?'

I knew perfectly well what he did. He was the swine who had been the 'administrator' of my band during the war, in other words he was a KGB officer. His job was to keep me inside Russia and it was right under his nose that I had escaped to join the Polish Army in

Persia. He wouldn't have forgotten that. Or forgiven it either. I often wondered what had happened to him when they found I had gone. Now I knew from Rosa that he hadn't been shot.

I felt the net tightening around me just as it had all those years ago. Would Rubinzik denounce me? Common sense told me that it wouldn't matter if he did. After all, the KGB must have known all about me before I made my first return to Russia. On the other hand Major Mozarin was already sniffing at my heels and such a denunciation might be all the KGB needed to hold me in Russia.

It was time to go. Any doubts I might have had were removed the day before we were due to leave for London, when Rosa once again returned to the subject. 'How exactly did you come to leave Russia during the war?'

I tried to sound casual. 'Oh, a lot of Poles wanted to join the Polish Army and since the Russians didn't think we were good enough to fight alongside the Red Army, they let us all go!'

'Oh,' said Rosa, 'I see . . .'

I began to think I had underestimated Rosa. I worried for the rest of that day and all the following day when we travelled out to the airport to fly home. I had gone through my baggage very carefully before leaving and I did not let my cases out of my sight once we had left the hotel. I had insisted that the performers took nothing with them but the simplest souvenirs.

As soon as we arrived at the airport I knew I had been right to take precautions. The customs had obviously been briefed and they pounced on us like vultures finding a fresh kill. They practically tore my suitcase to pieces and they turned my pockets inside out, even examining the stitching. While they searched us some men in civilian clothes kept up a running commentary through their walkie-talkies to someone unseen. The search went on and on, but finally the leader of the customs team looked at one of the men in the background and shrugged his shoulders. They conferred briefly on the radio before the civilian nodded in my direction. I could hear my heart accelerate.

The uniformed customs man walked over to me and looked at me in silence for a moment before he snapped: 'So you have nothing to declare, Comrade?'

'No,' I said, 'I have nothing to declare.'

'You're sure – no diamonds, no jewellery, no gypsy souvenirs?'

His taunt left me in no doubt that it was Mozarin who was in charge of this operation. I looked up and around instinctively, but could see nothing.

'No,' I said, 'I have nothing.'

To my surprise he let me through. And then called me back to give me my passport. I didn't breathe freely till we had landed and I walked on British soil once again. I had escaped from Russia for the very last time. I am never going back.

— EPILOGUE

Galina Brezhnev is now a woman of sixty. She lives in a private dacha in Shukovo near Moscow where a number of former Party functionaries of the Brezhnev era are housed. Her craze for diamonds and scandalous misuse of her position destroyed a large number of her friends, and those who did survive have by and large abandoned her. She is now excessively overweight and her clothes are shabby and worn. Most of her furs and fine dresses have been sold to subsidize her drinking habit.

Her husband Yuri Churbanov, having lost his position as First Deputy Minister of Internal Affairs, was given a minor post in the department, but subsequently lost his candidature for the Central Committee at the 27th Party Congress. In the spring of 1987 he was arrested and all his possessions were confiscated. In 1988 he went on trial accused of gross corruption and false acquisition of 650,000 roubles — about 270 years' salary for the average Soviet worker.

Towards the end of 1988 the news was leaked from Moscow that Boris Buryatsa had met his death only in the spring of 1988 — significantly just before the trial of Yuri Churbanov was announced. For years everyone had been led to believe that Boris had hanged himself shortly after his arrest in 1982, but the truth emerged that due to Galina's intervention and payment of huge bribes, Boris in fact received a five-year prison sentence and was released in 1987. But there were those for whom he remained a dangerous embarrassment, a potential threat to their own continued existence. Boris had to be silenced once and for all.

It is doubtful if Galina knows any of this. She does not read newspapers and is almost always drunk. She has been treated for alcohol addiction more than once, but to no effect. Occasionally, when darkness falls, she can be observed digging in the garden surrounding her dacha, searching for the diamonds and other treasures she supposedly buried there when she was first exiled.